MW00571854

TO Helen:

My dear co

Thank you to

in our family and for

accepting me in

the family. Thank

you for your

warm reception. May

the reading of this

work inspire

you and your

pursuits. May God

continue your

journey. Get

stronger,

stay

love

co...

Helen
ADO # N2d
MotHeR MAid
NAME
col b = Rd

Who Will *Lay* the First Stone—for an African-American Saint?

REVEREND ETHAN LAM, JR.
JULY 10 1939
DECEMBER 31 1996
PSALM 27:4

ETHAN LAM
PFC US ARMY
JULY 10 1939 ✝ DEC 31 1996
HUSBAND FATHER PASTOR
ROMANS 10: 9 & 10

Who Will *Lay* the First Stone—for an African-American Saint?

Chester Williams, Ph.D.

VANTAGE PRESS
New York

Cover design by Lesley Blakeney

FIRST EDITION

All rights reserved, including the right of
reproduction in whole or in part in any form.

Copyright © 2002 by Chester Williams, Ph.D.

Published by Vantage Press, Inc.
516 West 34th Street, New York, New York 10001

Manufactured in the United States of America
ISBN: 0-533-14011-0

Library of Congress Catalog Card No.: 01-130713

0 9 8 7 6 5 4 3 2 1

To Eddie:

My brother and friend

&

To Peter L. Berger:

One of the most brilliant minds of our times.
No one has influenced my intellectual and professional life
more.

Contents

Acknowledgments

In the ecclesiastical tradition of the African-American church, as well as my personal share in that tradition, I would be remiss not to *stand up and testify* of God's glory and mercy in completing another lap in the race. *Thank you, Lord.*

During the four years it took to write Ethan's story, James Williams repeatedly said to me that whether it was ever published or not, Ethan would be proud that I undertook the effort. When nothing else seemed able to push me past its many cognitive stalemates, this little dictum did. Others, without whose affirming presence the book would have remained an unintelligible assortment of disconnected fragments, are Sandra Sims Williams, Reverend Langford Floyd, Jane Frawley Zabielski, Lewis Brown Griggs, Dr. Patricia Piercy, Joy Williams, Erma Jenkins Watts, and Dr. William and Celeste Bennett. Denise Stinton, literary agent—though not for this piece—provided me a timely psychological lift when I was in one of those protracted writing doldrums writers typically go through. Her professional style, coupled with remarkable patience, integrity and comforting personalization with authors seeking her representation, was, as we say, *on the money.* I am especially thankful to Wilnette Dawodu Briggs who, upon receiving the first draft, was unable to put it down until the wee hours of the morning, as she put it. She found Ethan to be more than an indubitably righteous man: She saw him as a potential saint, simply dressed in righteous garb, as the case were. Needless to say, this revelation turned the book's thesis inside out. If James is right that Ethan would have been pleased with the motivations behind writing this story, I think he would have been equally satisfied with these friends' support of it. *Thank y'all.*

To my dear fellow laborers in the *Inner City and Africa Ministries'* Christian community of faith, those in Ghana, Senegal, Gambia, and Guinea Bissau, West Africa and in the continental United States, your sustaining and collaborative engagement in missions has been of inestimable moral and theological importance in the overall construction of the work, not to mention providing me a bit of much needed rhyme and reason in its development. *Merci!*

For the countless thousands whose lives Ethan touched, most of whom knew him well, and who concur that the record of his impeccable life, and sorrowful death and burial, have not been accorded accuracy, dignity, and decency, *Who Will* Lay *the First Stone—for an African-American Saint?* constitutes a small measure of closure. For, in a real sense, it is your story as much as it is his and mine, isn't it?

Finally, thank you Ann Thorpe for your technical assistance in the art display.

One of Ethan's lifelong theological passions was to get churches in which he was pastor to give 10% of their total income to global missions. That and more will be so donated in his memory from the book's sales. For information, and regarding Inner City & Africa Ministries' initiatives in general, call toll free, 1–866–440–ICAM (4226). E-mail: ICAM1985@aol.com.

Introduction

Following the Emancipation Proclamation, there was a mass exodus of African Americans from the south. Still breathing fumes from the smoldering ruins of slavery, poverty, and the civil war, these journeymen and women anxiously sought to reverse their dreadful social plight and the intolerable horrors of dehumanization. The political economy surrounding the first and second world wars would ignite subsequent migrations, also of those in pursuit of unrestricted social freedom, de-tyrannized communities in which to live and better economic opportunities for themselves and their children.

The paths of hope led them to rubber factories in Akron, automobile plants in Detroit, steel mills in Buffalo, and Pittsburgh, and other places thought to be better than from where they had come. Among these migrants were Mr. and Mrs. Ethan and Mary Lam, from Alabama and Georgia, respectively. The Lams settled in Pittsfield, a steel-mining town in western Pennsylvania, and had four children: Fred, Latha, Ethan Jr., and Jonathan.

This memoir is about one of them, Ethan Jr. He was my best friend; he died New Year's Eve, 1996.

Ethan's life was a tragic tale that highlighted the thinnest lines between love and hate, with him on their intersecting crests for more than thirty years. The book is not intended to be a definitive historical chronicle of his life, but a telling lesson on the juxtaposition of good and evil, of innocence and violation, etched onto the substance of that life. Inexplicably, Ethan's sojourn was pelted with a sustained barrage of accusation, punishment, and betrayal, principally from those he loved and trusted the most, a church in which he was pastor and a wife with whom he was in love. *Who Will*

Lay *the First Stone . . .* ? advances the hypothesis that he was a saint while on this draconian journey of pain and suffering.

I resolved to demystify Ethan's afflictions and to exhume his memory from the ash heaps of shame, including the construction of a surreptitious scheme to install a gravestone over his remains, fifteen months after his death.

The title of the memoir pivots off a morally insightful conversation that Jesus had with some unimpassioned critics of an adulterous woman in the first century. They wanted her to be stoned to death for being in violation of Mosaic Law, but he wanted her to live, to be whole, and to get on with her life. He took the spotlight they unsympathetically beamed on her and shined it back at them, coupled with a provocative reply, ". . . let him that is without sin, throw the first stone." Unable to defend their legalistic views on adultery and their own violations of the Law, they briskly walked away, murmuring defeatist obscenities under their breath as they went.

Of course, there are notable differences in the biblical story and this one, including characters, kinds of stones discussed, contexts and conclusions. That which gives them preliminary kinship is raising the questions who will *lay* . . . and who will *throw* and their respective remedies. The woman's accusers were told to proceed with the death-by-stoning punishment if they thought she was sinful and they weren't, which if they could have pulled it off would have been a deed of moral contradiction and disaffirmation. I, painfully restive because of my friend's stone-less grave, a post mortem emblem of his shamed life, sought moral retrieval. However successful I was or not, my pursuits were intended to be acts of affirmation.

While the story needles a thread of coherence around laying a stone over Ethan Lam, when it seemed there were no plans in the works to do so by anyone else, there is nothing particularly redeeming about such rituals. Some people actually think that letting "the dead bury the dead" is the best way to remember them and get on with life, whether it's the death of a friend, family, member or important notables. Others think that memorials, whether by way of enscripted stones or routine graveside visits, are obsessed with morbidity, maybe even fearful about one's own death prospective.

Psychologists view memorializing measures as enabling mechanisms for the surviving, as a way to negotiate emotionally destabilizing trauma induced by loss. Anthropologists, on the other hand, suggest that memorial rituals are important for the reintegration of customs and mores when death occurs, likening us to relay runners who are given the batons of ritual and tradition by the preceding generation, in order to pass them on to the succeeding one. Unchecked malfunctioning in the hand-off procedures could do irreparable harm to individuals, groups, and societies, they say.

For the religiously inclined, especially those in the Judeo-Christian tradition, memorials and stones are symbolic gestures of spiritual and moral remembering, whether enacted collectively or individually. As an example of the former, in the Old Testament, God tells Joshua to have twelve men from each of the tribes of Israel take an equal number of stones from the middle of the Jordan River when crossing. These stones were to serve as a lesson for inquisitive future generations on the miraculous parting of the waters for unimpeded passage.

In the New Testament, a more personal memorial, Jesus says of a poor woman who met up with him in at a mutual friend's house, she would have her act of love, sensitivity, and sacrifice memorialized, wherever in the world the gospel was preached. He gave her this tribute because she thought more of him, by anointing his tired body with expensive oils, than she did of herself, of others, or of worthy charities. Who Will *Lay* the First Stone . . . ? is nearer to that of this woman, in that it is a response of devotion to a friend. It is a friend whose journey the writer sought to anoint with dignity, to give him a cup of cool water when he was tired and weary in the heat of battle.

Most scripts of gender mistreatment center on women getting their worst and most persistent shares. This one is about a man who got his portion. In no way is it to be construed as female bashing or "reverse abuse"; nor does it seek to elicit sympathy for Ethan, a point on which I have been chided. After letting a friend review the work before its publication, a woman who has lived in a conjugally growth inhibiting relationship for years indicated that she would shed no tears for Ethan; that he, essentially, had the power to extricate himself from his pathos. What she was pointing out was her perception of the incomparable inequality in her journey and his, that hers was far worse. Knowing her views and activities on behalf of women, I suspect that she also had in mind the skewed proportion of their disenfranchisement as compared to men. In any case, I offer no rebuttal to her and others whose fight is to bring attention to the reckless plight of women. While suffering and abuse are ubiquitous in the human family, they are not evenly distributed, nor democratic in their manifestations.

Theological language and structures of knowledge punctuate most of the presentation, conceptually hugging its jagged borders. Among those terms that guide its theses are reconciliation, healing, grace, forgiveness, and of course, saint. However, *covenant* and *church* are its most important constructions, because they inform its moral centers, its turning, twisting angles of synthesis, contradiction, and disintegration.

For our purposes, covenants underscore relationships as binding, with a transcendent—if not holy—meaning that cannot be disavowed, dishonored, or forgotten. They are not to be confused with trendy religious rhetoric that bastardizes their biblical origins. In these cases, proponents hail them as special revelations from God to which they have exclusive interpretation, flailing them around the nation's pulpits, television stages, and tent microphones to demonstrate competitive advantage on ecclesiastic authenticity.

Regarding the church, there is little doubt that in the overall memoir of the African American community, it is seminal and irrevocable. Though its beliefs and actions have not been a monolithic voice of purpose, methodology and vision, more than any other institution, it has permeated the lives of black people in America. It is in their music, is the rhythm of their talk, is in the speeches of their leaders, bears the brunt of their jokes, is the first sought in times of personal and corporate difficulty and is, paradoxically, the most prolific source of their dissension. Even some of its harshest critics, such as leaders and followers of the Nation of Islam, have been said by the noted historian, John Henrik Clark, to be disgruntled Baptists.

In our story it initially appears as a place that black Pittsfielders are seen as going to, consistently more than any other. It shows up in the script as a segregating sanctuary, disallowing one its members a return to give thanks, is later defended in conversation with one its critics, and reappears as training ground for a youth directed religious renaissance. It is the place that *birthed* the narrative's principal character, Ethan Lam, Jr. *ordained* him as Reverend Ethan Lam, Jr., and *collaborated* in persecuting him to death as Reverend Ethan Lam, Jr., saint. Even though it's the ward on which I too was born, bred, and will be forever connected, I take swipes at it throughout the memoir. I do so for how it derisively mishandled Ethan, as well as for its glaring mismanagement of theology, acting beneath its calling, possibilities, and opportunities.

Despite its omnipresent religiosity, *Who Will* Lay *the First Stone* . . . ? has a message for non-religious persons. *For men whose fears and inhibitions interfere with their ability to embrace enduring relationships with other men,* it provides useful illustrations on individuation and courage. It suggests that they can un-apologetically and lovingly be their brother's keeper, their friend, their uncle and their father—until and after death does them part.

The narrative has a thought *for persons suffering prolonged agony;* that their families and friends may be able to look at them differently—not as victims doomed to a life of hopeless misery, but as possible saints called to exemplary take the rest of us higher. Reading about Ethan may not abate pain and discomfort, but his story could very well center a level of meaning, heretofore, undisclosed.

For those in search of selfless love, Ethan's examples of it, as well as its fellow attributes, tolerance and mercy, leap off every page of his storied life. He clearly wanted nothing in return for the love he so generously gave to those he met, except in the case of his wife and marriage, evidence that it was a forever affair.

For husbands and wives who find themselves on the short end of their marriage covenants, the book is a reminder that unless love vows, fidelity, and respect are consciously and regularly revisited, theirs could be a life of emotional and spiritual paralysis.

Because its principal messages are more likely to appeal to religious communities, it has an exhortation for denominational adherents, *those that permit the emergence of power*

brokers to tinker with the theological arrangements between them-
selves and their God, between their pastor and their world. It is,
"God *don't* like ugly."

Its chapters unfold in Pittsfield, PA, though its panoply
of themes spans the lives of people living all across the continental United States, especially African Americans. Most
black communities have their Worcester Avenues, their Pekins Woods, and their Queen Esther's houses, people and
places found on the "Back in the Day" pages that illuminate
the black cultural adage, " . . . everything is everything."

I have assigned the book's characters and locations fic-
titious identities, in order to shield the innocent, as well as
others whose entries appear uncomplimentary. I have tried
to hang a protective veil over Ethan's children, as well as over
Ethan, *lui-meme.* The most troublesome of this clandestine
maneuvering is the book's focus on Mrs. Lam; it is an inherently unavoidable, if not pestiferous attachment.

Its contents reflect a composite reconstruction of my
childhood and teenage memories, an interpreted compila-
tion of intensive conversations that I had with Ethan over
the years, and selective interviews with people who knew
him well.

Finally, I am a Christian, serving God in West Africa;
however, this work is not an evangelistic or missionary mono-
graph, nor a treatise on pastoral care. It is a script written in
defense of a brother, couched in a personal and theological
friendship that is as vibrant after his death as it was when he
lived. Some of my fellow Christians may find its publication
objectionable, by virtue of its unrestrained intrusion into
places they regard as holy, private, and untouchable—the
family. Others may take umbrage with its constructions of a
social history at variance with their views of spiritual conversion, namely, with the " . . . forgetting those things that are
behind . . . " injunctions in the Bible. To these Christians, I

espouse a view of integrated faith and its expression of real-life events prior to and succeeding that conversion. I am only sorry that I may not have written this piece well enough so as not be offensive to them if they think differently, and I regret any subsequent discomfort it may cause as a result.

1

Who Will *Lay* the First Stone . . . ?
Its Anatomy

The Ethan Lam Jr. story deserves being told because of its nexus to some of history's harshest portrayals of persecution and dehumanization. The intersecting trails of disgrace and obfuscation in Ethan's tumultuous life to theirs are noteworthy. In some ways they are a classic example of "why bad things happen to good people." In others, due to the deliberately inflicted obstacles untidily placed around him, they represent a much more fascinating problem of theodicy.

I confess that the scripted lines of Ethan's life produce a disturbing sense of alienation—me, writing about my deceased friend, when in several conversations we had before he died, we talked about doing some writing together. We were to have taken a look at the African American church and its global improbabilities, something I will have to now do with him in absentia, as posthumus editor. I have swung back and forth on the "write" and "don't write" pendulum, on whether to record the startling events of my friend's journey, or to simply chalk it all up to *c'est la vie* misfortune. I have chosen the former. I have also vacillated between how much I could say that would not compromise the sanctity of his "please don't mention it" disclosures, and how little I could say so as to not excoriate, embarrass, or hurt those he loved. I have been as discreet as I could, uneasily tiptoeing along their points of forbidden entry.

My tension has been exacerbated by a dispute over who and how the management of his memory is to be conducted—on which point, my agenda is clear, to give the widest possible readership to his quintessential life and rewrite the back page clips of his death. This conflict is not unique, of course. Squabbles over inheritances, money, and who gets the family dog and '73 Chevrolet have been known to rip families apart not long after the final funeral Amen and closing of the coffin lid. There is presently a court dispute in Atlanta, Georgia, over the speeches of Dr. Martin Luther King, Jr. The debate centers on whether they are private property, and therefore not marketable for profits without family approval and entitlements, or whether they belong to the larger public domain, to be made available to it upon demand.

I have concluded that while memories may be the moral properties of families who lay tenacious claim to them, they do not hold their exclusive rights, resolutely so if those in question have significantly impacted history and the lives of others. If Sojourner Truth's family requests that no symposia be convened to honor her memory, for example, they would likely be ignored and as unrelated to Sojourner at all if the truth were told. Some may even think them to be a bit wacky. We can only hope when battles exist over how the dead are to be remembered, when inquirers start snooping around the rooms that house their pleasant and less than pleasant memories, that their pursuits will be honest and truthful, and reflect a conscious regard for the integrity of the facts.

In the aftermath of Ethan's death, I have carefully reviewed the broken covenants and unforgiving betrayals in his life, and I have painstakingly searched the records to make sense of it all. I have been deliberately cautious in this undertaking, seeking to ensure that my endeavors would not constitute merely a therapeutic exercise of a friend unable to cope.

One thing was certain: I knew I needed to segregate reasonable anger from constraints of objectivity, and to deal with the business of vengeance and vindictiveness as possible backlashes. Regarding these reactions, I have been guided most of my life by the theology that where ruthless deeds and senseless acts of misdirected rage exist, such as I think was the case with Ethan, that God would ultimately handle their perpetrators, that He would balance the books of justice. Simply, I was taught, retribution and judgment are things with which we need not concern ourselves. They are things that *God does*—stated in biblical terms, " . . . vengeance is mine, sayeth the Lord . . . "

Vindictiveness, on the other hand, is a pathological level of twisted thinking that motivates individuals to settle the score with the purveyors of bad deeds, an emotionally and spiritually useless expenditure, for sure. Those in serious pursuit of psychological and spiritual wholeness are best advised to avoid its costly consequences.

Vindication is yet another question; it is aimed at setting the record straight. It is engagement of intentional righteousness that God has placed within arms' reach of the human family. It is what *we do*. Whether for the innocently accused, for exploited and disadvantaged groups, or for self-serving victimization of, say, "racial, ethnic and gender others," vindication is an incontestably judicious and conscionable act with which we befriend the innocent, weak, and defenseless—sometimes, others, sometimes ourselves.

Commensurate with my salient literary objective to switch the image of Ethan's life from ridicule to sainthood, *Who Will* Lay *the First Stone* . . . ? is a kind of vindication, proposing to set his life and death accounts straight. There are basically three things that sequentially and cumulatively impacted my decision to write it. None would have been singularly, or in combination with only one other, sufficient to do so.

The *first* is connected to the awful feeling of incompletion I had when learning of his death, and the decision that his funeral would proceed whether or not I was present. I was in West Africa upon hearing the news, and so desperately wanted and needed to be present; but international plane scheduling from developing countries is not as cooperative as when traveling within the continental United States. I would arrive in Pittsfield a few hours after the internment.

I have often experienced the awful sting of my pain. I couldn't view my friend's remains nor take my place with others in saying farewell. I didn't have the opportunity to ceremonially participate in shouldering his coffin along that interminably long corridor, down the church aisle, and out to the waiting hearse at the curb. These gnawing, gut-wrenching feelings of emptiness were compounded by the precipitous annulment of a teen-age covenant that Ethan and I had repeatedly made over the years. Namely, whoever died first, the other would preach his funeral, a fact well known to nearly everyone in the African American church community in Pittsfield.

The days immediately preceding and following his funeral were some of the darkest I've known. My bestfriend was dead, and unlike good friends who are more easily replaceable, best friends are not. They are gone forever. If I could have only said Amen when hearing the appointed minister celebrate some aspect of his appealing life, or read a Bible verse about his good fight of faith, or sung a line of one of his favorite songs, I would have been all right. I think. I could do neither of these. I just couldn't *get to the church on time,* and the funeral processional couldn't wait, or something . . .

Since then, I have thought that it might have been just as well for me not to be in attendance. For how could I have sat quietly in a pew seat while someone else had been given the preaching assignment, someone who was quite innocent and willing but having only bits and pieces of the story?

Listening to the various recitations, could I have done like the biblical character, John the Baptist, and wrapped myself in camel hair while biting down on a few wild locusts and honey, in this case to show my dissent? Could I have defiantly stood up in the sanctuary and asked for a halt to the service, when not hearing in the labyrinth of eulogy highlights the life of righteousness he so wonderfully led, things with which I knew I was more familiar? Well, the answer is probably no to all these questions, but in my disconnected state of pummeling anguish, I submit how far my thoughts had taken me.

The *second* was that more than a year after Ethan's burial, there was no stone at his grave site, only institutional section and plot numbers to identify the location of his remains. It was as though he never lived or died, sort of like *the grave of the unknown saint.* To leave him stripped of honor like this was outside all I knew about cultural and religious protocol; it was definitely not that with which I would be personally content. I knew that I would have to take action. With speaking engagement money, about $650, I had a monument made, personally dug a hole in Bardale's cemetery grounds, and planted it over Ethan's coffin.

A few weeks later, it was deliberately cracked and uprooted. This was the *third* reason for wanting to tell Ethan's story, the broken stone. It wasn't just the fact of its removal, but that someone had taken a blunt instrument, a sledgehammer or rock, and broke it into pieces, beforehand. So, my brother was buried in a nameless burial plot on an unlit outer edge of a cemetery; then my effort to reface him with memory and respect, in laying the stone, was met with such disgrace, such desecration. There was a quiet but controlled rage inside of me. I felt like the uneasy but tireless servant, who when commanded by his detractors to sit down, adamantly replied, " . . . no, I can't sit down . . . " a lyric of resolve that found its way into my song: I wouldn't either—sit down, I am talking about.

I have been sternly scolded for crossing the line in doing what I understand only family members are authorized to do—lay gravestones over their members—and for my insistence on making the Ethan Lam story public. I have heard such remarks as, "Why don't you leave him alone? He wouldn't like all this fuss being made over him." "He is surely in heaven: Let his body rest in peace." And then there is that perennial question if Ethan would have approved the writing of the narrative. Whether the fuss I have generated in Ethan's story is excessive, or if I should let him rest in peace when, notwithstanding his faith journey, he didn't live or die in this state, I am not altogether certain. One thing of which I am sure, that the poorly and inaccurately scripted pages of his life must be written to meet the requirements of truth, honor, and dignity.

The issue of whether he would have stamped his endorsement on the book is also one I cannot answer. I suspect he would have shied away from accolades pointing to his acts of goodness, as well as those depicting him as a maligned subject of abuse. He would have most assuredly resisted disparaging inferences of his family, and he would have been torn between his sense of justice and truth, and his predilection to love those who mistreated him, brutally, unjustly, and unfairly. Given the awfully private person that he was, and the lengths to which he went to subvert discussions of his own sexuality, I think he would have scoffed at the book's references to his costly mis-education and reluctance to openly talk about the subject—sex.

Contrary to the extraordinarily righteous person he was, an unlikely candidate to air the underside of his life, I make

6

no self-claim of sainthood, and I know of no one who would submit my name for canonization. Without being irreverent, pompous, or cocky, it is *I* that have chosen to write about him, to exonerate his life, to reveal his glorious sensibilities and the vicious ways in which they were exploited.

In writing of his life, I have eased my way past its various "do not enter signs," though I have not intended to be a mere pesky meddler in the lives of those lured into its seemingly unforgiving embrace. I have only intended to show Ethan's eminent gifts of grace and his exalted way of thinking and behaving, to raise his sainthood out of the stench-corroded dirt in which it was buried. In that process, and in my occasional frenzied shoveling up grave dirt that covers his face, I may have inadvertently soiled the clothes of those standing near the mouth of the grave with shovels filled with dirt of their own—frantically throwing them in a downward trajectory.

2

Back in the Day

It's the late 1950s, in Pittsfield, PA. This period and the events it birthed formed the backdrop in which the city's values, ideas, and beliefs emerged of that day, defining the parameters for how Ethan and I would dialectically interact with them.

Pittsfield is the home of The Kids' Derby, an event testing children's skills in building and racing fuel-less wooden cars, of The World Series of Tennis, an August classic, and of "Rehab Anonymous," an international organization for recovering drug abusers. It is the home of singers, "Ruby and The Romancers," of Olympian, and former world record holder in the 400-meter run, Butchie Renaud, and of Gus Jackson and Nate Theisman, National Basketball Association Hall of Fame enrollees.

The Cathedral Church, when initially built in an adjacent suburb, was billed as the largest church in the world. It was stouted with the Pittsfield Baptist Temple that boasted of having the largest Sunday school in the world. Unfortunately, the Temple was also quietly reputed to frown upon blacks coming in numbers more than a few at a time, and made it clear that their visiting was preferred over their joining. Had the New Testament's Apostle Paul dropped in on this western Pennsylvania City, he might have said of it, " . . . I perceive that you are religious . . ."

Pittsfield was widely thought of as the steel capital of the world and was the place to which African Americans came en masse from the economically depressed South.

They, along with others, would invest their dreams in Pittsfield's steel mills, only to years later see them turned into nightmares as a result of automation, plant relocation, and "for profits only" decision making.

Whatever was in store for the future Pittsfield, its '50s, '60s, and early '70s version was an oasis of opportunity and hope. Factory jobs were plentiful, houses were relatively cheap, and black communities were dancing to the joyous music of a new daydawning. On the west side of town where our families lived, Ethan's and mine, neighborhoods were thriving. Within a radius of four city blocks on Worcester Avenue, one of the city's integrative hubs of cultural and business activity, there were three drug stores, three supermarkets, and several smaller grocery outlets. There were also product-specific outlets selling fresh bottled milk, fresh fish, vegetables and fruits, and live poultry that store keepers would kill and dress while you watched and waited.

There were four bakeries on the avenue: each kept us well supplied with delectable pastries, including two-for-a-nickel "day old" cookies. We didn't always know exactly how old they were, and we didn't really care. I just remember that they were always in abundant supply, as we made our daily visits to get them. With Ike's Ice Cream Parlor conveniently located, selling nice size cones for a dime, we sometimes ate so much of both until we were crazy.

Worcester Avenue was a corridor of irresistible attraction to all who dared to enter and experience it. Whether walking its beat by day or standing on its corners by night, we could feel its swaying magic, like cool evening breezes negotiating the intolerable discomforts of the city's hot summer nights. The revolving turnstile that moved us in and out of its unharnessed moods of ecstasy brought us face to face with the best and, occasionally, the worst in us.

Our entries and exits to the avenue's festive rhythms were not to be denied. We talked, laughed, and jostled each other from one end to the other, from the time it opened until the time it closed. The best cut, the shiniest shoes, the best pressed and curled hair, the sharpest creased pants and balloon, hula hoop skirts, and the stiffest starched shirts could all be done at Morton's Barber and Beauty Salon, Hector's Shoe Shine Parlor, and Al's Cleaners. Week in and week out, these establishments embellished us for another Saturday night and Sunday morning " . . . feel like sanctified . . . " activities.

Old and young alike brought mythical badges of distinction on the avenue, "Arrow Lip," "Beak," "Mickey," "Baby Brother," "Slick" and "Nose." They called me "Terrible," or should I say I begged people to. "Terrible" was my bravado self-designation, suggesting that I possessed the edge in outdueling my peers in jive stuff. The truth is, I put little fear in the weak and was a joke to the strong. Seeing a blimp for the first time, shortly after our arrival from the coal fields of West Virginia, and screaming to the top of my lungs because I thought it was a bomb, didn't enhance my image of being all that terrible.

Most of the city's youth were members of social clubs. I joined the *Jr. Crusaders,* a division of an older group bearing the same name. Its membership included "hanging out," an ability to hold your own in "signifying" (demeaning rhetoric about family relations), and a willingness to engage in a little light deviant behavior from time to time. After a gang fight that resulted in a couple of unattractive-busted lips, and an overnight stay at a youth detention center, I relinquished my membership in the club.

I sought alternative reference groups in which to define myself. Louis D. Wimsly, Clistene Fason, Clinton Lee, Sandra Shils, Mayme Stephens and others would help me appreciate

10

pursuing academic excellence as much, if not more, as hangin' out. While I was never awarded the city's most outstanding intellectual youth plaque, being on this new track with friends who were among some of its brightest students placed a little sway in my step.

But Pittsfield was more than its west side, its Worcester Avenues, and its social clubs. It was a place that brought African Americans together, citywide.

On Saturday mornings, at *Simmel Beach Amusement Park*, black youth came to show off their dextrous roller-skating abilities. Charles Athens and company flipped and flew through the air like gazelles, dazzling us more floor-bound mortals with their exploits. They did on wheels, high above floor level, what Michael Jordan does with a basketball there—dance, dance, dance. After skating and a few falls and knockdowns on rink floors, if we had money left over, we would buy sticks of cotton candy, a couple of nickel bags of popcorn, and ten cent soda pops. We would ride the bump cars, the roller coaster, and Ferris wheel, and climax the day with a lot of laughs when looking at grotesque representations of ourselves in large mirrors near the park's exit. The standing joke was that these distorted appearances actually made some of us look better.

On Sunday afternoons, the guys I moved with, "homeboys," either went horse riding at Idal's Riding Academy or to the downtown show—the Palatial, Colon, Stran, or Loews, where we usually sneaked in through the theater's exit-only doors. We rarely saw the feature, rather chose to get our kicks by throwing paper missiles at patrons while we crunched on Milk Duds and Good and Plenty candies. If we were lucky to have our girlfriends present, and we tried not to leave it to luck, draping an arm around her shoulder as we smacked and crackled on them—the Milk Duds and Good and Plenty, I mean—was the highlight of the evening.

11

At Idal's, I always rode the horse, "Old Red," until one day she decided to take me full speed through the academy's wooded area without heeding my rein-pulls and prayerful pleas to stop. After getting off the ground, massaging bruises on areas on my body never seen by other humans, my horseback riding days were numbered. Falling on your backside on a skating rink wooden floor was not quite the same as being thrown from a horse to the earth's ungiving surface, especially after having been hit in the face a few times by tree branches while in transit. Needless to say, it didn't take much for me to stay with those activities in which I had just a tad more control.

It is hard to fathom that we paid $1 an hour to gallop horses over the plains, hills and slopes, when in today's horse-riding economy, it costs $15 per hour to just walk 'em on a few trails. Cheers for the good old days.

One of the most important social arenas of meaning in Pittsfield was *Pekins Woods,* sometimes just called "the park." This was a place for blacks to display their seasonal fashions and to just gather, sit and sit, and chitchat and smile. It was the rustic hideaway where lovers met and strolled its naturally manicured paths of beauty. It was the home of the Rens, a nearly unbeatable softball team that earned crowd-standing ovations from their scores of fans on Sunday afternoons, and it was the showcase for George "Bones" Gilman. George could make incredibly melodious music by banging two sticks together between his fingers, (called the "bones") while captivating his audience with a smile that stretched the length and breadth of the park.

Pekins Woods housed the tennis courts of brothers Bernie and Bithan Boyer and of Ethan Parks. These racket swingers used to make us dizzy as they yo-yoed our heads back and forth, hitting balls across the nets at lightning speed. Up the hill from the courts, the smooth ball-handling of basketball players thrilled spectators from around the city, while various male "doo wop" groups crooned in the background underneath Pekins' shady trees. We could always count on the brothers to do a little light harmonizing. Some were very good, while others were very bad; so much so that they made you want to smack 'em for mauling and mugging this time-honored music tradition in the African American community.

Once in a while, an individual talent would take front stage, such as William Jefferson, who, with a little training, could have easily been a successful operatic talent. But with the military experience having early on gotten to his mind, and alcohol later on to his body, his venues were limited to park appearances, an occasional lead vocal in St. James's church choir, and late-night serenades in the neighborhood. I once threw a shoe out of our attic window at his head, when at 2:00 A.M. one morning he was singing "Santa Lucia" to the top of his lungs. Like too many "young, gifted and black" artists, William died before time, depriving the world of enhanced joy.

Next to the park was the *custard stand,* a place you dared not come anywhere near without getting a cone of its deliciously soft ice cream, a frosty milk shake, and a tasty foot-long hot dog—one combination to eat at the time and one to go. This little food parlor did more than satisfy our eating appetites; it served as a neat little commentary on the stratification of African American teens. Particularly after a big sporting event or dance, hundreds of us would gather to profile, each clamoring and jockeying around the *stand* for prominent position. Athletic prowess, popularity, dress, and good looks were among those variables that identified not only where others saw us into the pecking order of importance, but where we saw ourselves.

The singular most important measure of status was the car we drove. With dangling fox tails, shining hub caps, spotless white side wall tires, brightly lit reflectors attached to wheel flaps, back bumpers lowered as near to the ground as possible and a scented tree for mood meant that you were "in the house"—or "in the car," as the case was. For added machismo, dudes pulled their ladies next to them, moved over to the middle of the car in the "Cleveland lean," and "got rubber" as they sped away. If that didn't bring on the final rush, lifting the already standing audience to its feet, the ritual would be reenacted at the next custard-stand gathering.

Mixers were another happening that brought us together. From surrounding towns, Kenston, Rabanna, and Barberthon, African American youth would weekly join Pittsfielders for "hot fun in the summer time" jamming, each impacting the other with their own styles of slang and hip hop. As sky-flying roller skaters took our breath away when dancing on wheels, some of the city's best dancers, Will Feton, Lynn Debaney, and Albert Paul electrified mixer crowds with their slick feet and body movements on converted gymnasium floors. Alex Mobey was usually off in one corner conducting clinics on the cha, cha, cha, while Louis D. Wimsly was off in another, showing spectators how to do the "shuffle." In its routine, you needed a 14 1/2 shoe size, Lou's foot size—at age 14—to get the real feel of the floor, as it stubbornly moved under your foot patting, sliding gyrations.

Mixers were especially colorful when football stars Bob Clark, Tracy Dingel, Robert Garkett, and Earl Quinny, co-starring majorettes, Shirl Gordon and Melda Tolibet, made their entrance. These hometown celebrities thought that they were cute, as did the rest of the city, having dazzled us with their running and choreographed stepping at a game earlier in the day and on the dance floor at night.

Guys would typically swagger in late to the mixer, sporting razor-sharp, creased pants about eight inches above their waistlines. They would wear winged-tipped shoes with enough shine to light up a dark night. How high they rose on their toes when walking, pushing noticeably off from their heels, was an indication of how cool they thought they were. You could always distinguish the walking patterns of black guys from white ones by the number of feet used for push-up walking. White guys pushed off and up on both feet. Black guys did so on only one, as though one leg was physically impaired or limp.

Shorter guys, whether African American or white, pushed off from both feet, planting each foot after the other as high as they could, on as many legs as they had or could borrow. They wanted to appear tall with every opportunity. In their glory when platform shoes came into vogue, there was great mourning among men under 5 feet 4 inches after they went out. You would have thought there was an embargo on hair grease.

If it was a social occasion that required formal dress, male teens could be seen nervously pulling at their jacket sleeve, right hand fingers clasping in back of the right sleeve and left hand fingers in back of the left. This was more a hip gesture of fashion than a phobic fear that shirt cuffs would embarrassingly slip into view. Brothers always tried to be as distinguishably cool as they could, capitalizing on everything from what they wore to how they wore it, to where and how they drove their cars, to what and how they said things to each other.

When taking their act to the dance hall, and when the disc jockey rived up the old mixer turntable, dudes would disinterestedly place their wide brim Stetson hats into the hands of a waiting sister and waltz her around the floor. If it was to a fast record, she gracefully swung the carefully creased hat up and down in the routine, proudly swirling it in the air as a kind of badge of identification, distinction, and honor. If she happened to have been with a social notable and/or her boyfriend, her arms grew noticeably longer and her swings increasingly wider. She wanted the world to take note of her and the man with whom she danced.

When couples swooned to slow tunes, the sister would gently hold the hat on her partner's back, as she buried her heavily rouged face on his clean shirt. When the music ended, she would either grudgingly return the Stetson or hold on to it for the night. This was a signal to other sisters that the hat owner was taken—for interested brothers, she was.

The smaller versions of mixers were Friday night, fifteeem-cents-for-admission, *house parties*. These party-down affairs were often held in rooms where at least seventy more people would crowd in than they were made for. Had the fire marshall ever made unannounced visits to some of these houses, they would have surely shut them down, probably not even permitting their residents re-entry.

Queen Esther was known to throw some of the best, especially those mid-afternoon sessions to which we secretly couldn't wait to get to when playing hooky. With lights so low that you needed sun glasses to see the person standing next to you, and body steam so pronounced that you could cut its formations with a knife, "In the Still of the Night" and "Your Precious Love" danced party goers into near hypnotic moods of bliss. As crowds hid themselves in basements' thick dark mists, much to the delight of the males in attendance, dancing was pretty much limited to its slower art forms.

16

Black and White Pluko was a hair-curling oil used by black women, as was Murrays, Supergroom, and Tuxedo pomades by black men. Neither felt fully dressed unless the hair was slicked, waved, and curled with several ounces. I never thought I would miss African American women's hair aroma until I went away to predominately white schools and was unable to experience it. When coming home for holidays and summer recesses, I couldn't wait to just bury my nose in a sister's hair, didn't matter whose.

Along with guys naturally humping their hair with these odorized lards were the chemicals they used for more radical hairstyles, " . . . and now, . . . introducing to some and presenting to others . . . " *conks and processes.* The former could best be described as the (old) Little Richard look, the latter, Nat King Cole's. Cheap and cheaper colognes, a little body musk from heavy dancing action, and these hair scents and styles confirmed the hunch that you were ready to party.

Recording artists, the Clovers, Dominoes, Frankie Lyman, Little Anthony and the Imperials, Ruth Brown, Big Mabelle, the Moon Glows, and Johnnie Ace sang us up to "cloud nine." Others taking us there were the home spun melodious voices of the Emerauds, the Turbins and Ruby Nashly. They actually took us further, sometimes to outer galactic frontiers, as they rocked the house on talent night and at house parties and mixers. Their silky smooth harmonies and soothingly soft voice blends brought rhapsody to the city. They were our talents, and we took pride in them.

We similarly did so when Eugene Huntley "brought the bacon home" with one of his rare wins in the boxing ring, when Frankie Montgoms and M.J. Johnson streaked past runners in the 100-yard dash, and when Clinton Leigh and Jack Lomar ran the hurdles at track meets. These dash men were like ballet dancers in fast forward, they were. We screamed ourselves into hysteric fits when they strutted their stuff. Pittsfield gave birth to gifted white athletes during this period, too. Jimmy Dar had the sweetest jump shot in town, and Glen J. David was one of the fastest humans to ever run track. We had nothing but admiration for them and other whites who were good at what they did.

As is the case with most African American communities, that institution that gave us hope to keep pace with our moral destiny was the church. When there was no other place to go, and when there was every other place to go, the church was that singularly special place where African Americans inevitably went. Its ringing bells signaled that it was time for Sunday morning service, for mid-week Bible study and prayer meeting, for Tuesday night choir rehearsal, and for deacon, trustee board, BYPTU and YPWW meetings.

The beliefs and liturgical differences that existed between Pittsfield's black churches, then, reinforced in their private celebrations, were inconsequential. The broader religious call bringing us together had an inspiringly effective way of cutting through them, lifting congregants to the highest plateaus of denominationally integrated enrichment.

Pittsfield had a gifted number of African American clergy. Reverend Eugene Morton, pastor of Wesley Institutional African Methodist Episcopal Zion Church, for decades, was among its most eloquent. I was recently reminded that his eulogy for Mrs. Hazel Wright lives on. Of her he sermonized, "The Music Is Gone, But the Melody Lingers on." This homily will still preach in the tradition of African American homiletics, " . . . *right where I stand.*"

As neighboring Aliquippa had its Nelsons, Wards, and Hoovers, rocking black churches in "on the wings of the morning," Pittsfield had its Shils, Lincolns, Fowler, Smiths, Williamses, Upshils, Burrows, and Humphreys. It also had Sister Geraldine Peterkin, Mothers Nel, Pete, and Scott, Bishops Ash, Drolls, and Robins, and Elders Kirk, Jefferson, Hill, and McCurray. When for some reason they couldn't "take us to the mountain," they invited Horace Shepherd from Philadelphia, Missouri Gray from Gary, and members of the Cleveland family from Los Angeles to help them.

With different styles, theologies and approaches to ministry, these Pittsfield leaders embroidered protective patches of righteousness onto a mosaic shawl for us, warming us from the cold winds of evil, delusion, and deception. Now showing signs of wear, due to heavy usage in life's frigid deserts, the old shawl's protective warmth and guiding truths still sustain us.

Pittsfield, similarly, had an impressive array of gospel singers, including the Richard Street Church of God singers, Mt. Holly Gospel Chorus, the Wesley Institutional A.M.E. Zion Gospel Choir, the Richard Brad Singers, the Buch Brothers, the Lawson Kids, the Heavenly Journeymen, and the incomparable voice of Eugene Burkeman. With respect to Eugene, whether he was singing as soloist or as a member of the Lammond Stawberry Singers, he was an absolutely incredible gifted singer. When he sang, " . . . if when you give the best of your service, telling the world that the Savior has come," you felt like you had boarded a sacred car on Gladys Knight's train, though not the one going to Georgia: *that midnight train to glory.*

Nearly every Sunday a group of us who regularly ran together could be found at somebody's church anniversary or gospel singing program. We went without the benefit of air conditioning on hot summer afternoons or sufficient heat on cold winter ones. At all cost, we wanted to stay in fellowship with the saints. We sang and shouted far into the night, to employ a phrase from the catechism of the righteous, "until the power came down." None of this, "I've got to get up and go to work tomorrow" talk. When the last choir and musician had left, and the janitor had dragged us out of the sanctuary, kicking and screaming all the way to the door, we would top things off with a bit of celebration debriefing, munching on fast food sandwiches and soft drinks at local drive-ins. Without a doubt, those feet stompin' and hand clappin' "back in the day" times were downright good for the soul.

Like other African American cities, Pittsfield was sashaying to the music by the Caravans, James Cleveland, and the Roberta Martin Singers. The Caravans, under the inimitable leadership of Albertina Walker, brought a new and stirring gospel sound into our choir lofts. The moving rhythms and variations of their music was unlike any we had heard, yet was recognizable because it was studiously connected to the traditions preceding it. This trail blazing group of, mostly, women established a class of excellence that not many have gained admission in since. No gospel music library is complete without a Caravans' shelf.

James Cleveland reintroduced yet another element into the log of black gospel, the prominence of big church choir recordings. Of course, large choirs and their lead vocalists were not new in African American worship, but he brought a rendition of them that sent waves of praise throughout black communities. His recording with the Nutley, New Jersey Mass Choir of "Peace Be Still" was the standard by which choir singing would be measured for decades.

More than being just a musician, James Cleveland also seemed consciously aware of the need to make easily understood transitions within and between African American generations; he was a kind of gospel music anthropologist. He brokered new gospel forms in ways that older blacks could approvingly identify, and those that the younger ones could enjoy singing. Inter-generational continuity in black religious music was apparently as important to him as was what was being played and sung. When there existed doubt on the clarity of either, or whether it was a question of synchronizing preaching and music, he would stop singing and impromptu talk the message to and through black generations without warning or script, and without missing a beat. Asking them, " . . . Can I get a witness . . . ?" and reaching as far back into their experiences as necessary to draw common ground familiarity with culture and tradition, kept him religiously and anthropologically close to the sacredness of black church roots.

Despite this gospel renaissance, and despite the exhilaration of Simmel Beach and Pekins Park, et al, everything in Pittsfield was not spiritual bliss nor fun and games. Three, in succession, accidental teenage murders, a number of headline spousal-abuse cases, and a couple of notable domestic homicides rocked the city on its heels. Pittsfield also had its share of ganglike violence and cross-town brawling, with a small thug element that got their kicks from beating up people for the heck of it. The Miller Brothers in central Pittsfield, for example, were widely known for "throwing down," and they would do so in a heart beat if their reputation of "kings on the hill" was in doubt. If violence- or rumble-shy, one didn't exactly relish the idea of being in the same place as the Miller Brothers, or were reported to be en route.

The deeper problem in Pittsfield was the cyclical incongruity found at the heart of most African American urban communities, the lack of self-sufficiency in the economic sector. Shoe shine parlors, a few mom-and-pop stores, the ubiquitous presence of hair-dressing establishments, and an insurance company or two were the only enterprises owned by blacks. The larger businesses were owned by whites, regarding which fact, public reference or political dissent was rarely made. Complaints were usually limited to ethnic and racial name dropping, and that, in the privacy of blacks' homes upon discovering that we had been short changed at the cash register or sold a slab of bad meat.

At the level of personal redress, never enough for reversing institutionalized inequalities, I recall my matriarchal Aunt Pinkie escorting me to Speck's Supermarket for a job when I was about twelve. Her persuasive argument to store owners was that she had patronized Speck's for years and wanted her nephew to have a work opportunity there. They then hired and paid me $3 per week, though they paid my bag-packing colleagues $15 and $18. Having earned $2.35 a day on nearby township farms, and $5 a day for heavy construction details, I thought it was just the way things were. Aunt Pinkie, when learning of the real deal at Speck's, made another trip to the store's management. As she had initially dressed me up when taking me to get the job, she undressed them when learning that they were exploiting me. She made me quit, and lobbied for me another job at a downtown hotel.

There existed other Aunt Pinkies around Pittsfield in those days, as there are countless numbers around the nation, women and men who are hewn from Gibraltar's rock. Unfortunately, they don't get together frequently enough to make their courageous and righteous voices heard.

3

The Making of a Saint

Ethan Lam was born in August, 1943, to a working class
Christian family noted for its values of hard work and sacrifice. He was short in stature, about 5 feet 8 inches, and probably never weighed more than 120 pounds, soaking wet. He
wasn't a terribly imposing person, in fact, was often weak,
frail, and sickly. When a teen, he contracted sugar diabetes,
the stage that required daily insulin injections. But despite
this limitation and lack of physical prowess, Ethan early on
showed signs of unusual moral character.

It is not customary to think of saints and their canonization outside of the Roman Catholic tradition, least of all
of African Americans as such. I recently asked a woman in
Pittsfield if she regarded Mother Teresa as a saint. She indicated that she did, but she exploded at the thought of my
speaking of her and extraordinarily righteous African Americans in the same breath. There is no doubt that the rules
and norms of interpretation that determine African Americans to be sinners are on the opposite side of the page that
determine them to be saints or saint worthy.

Saints are individuals having exceptional amounts of
grace, kindness, and mercy, and bear distinctive resem-
blance to things divine. Some grow into their sainthood naturally; some are induced into it supernaturally, while others
may be pulled into its ranks through cataclysm or misfortune. Those ascribed its virtues are typically not restrained
by normative structures of behavior; they tend to do good
even when reason and circumstance call for a different response. They are generally thought of as "holier than us,"

though they never think of themselves in this manner, as "holier than thou."

Without a revisionist stretch of history and definition, this descriptive apparel can be wrapped around the life of Ethan. Those who knew him will attest to the fact that he was a highly moral and spiritual human being who gracefully commanded their attention; most can't seem to remember when he wasn't this awfully righteous person they deeply respected and cherished, were even awed by. He was a devout Christian, conceived in the womb and grew up marching to the cadence of the Mount Holly Baptist Church. He was active in its Sunday School, taught its adult Bible classes as a youth, and would have it said by Reverend Haynes, its senior minister, that he had great ministry potential.

I recall having been attracted to his pious demeanor and precocious approach to Christian theology. He was introspective, though not in a self-absorbed or mystical sense, and he had a remarkable ability for administering structures of resolution for the lowly and disinherited. He possessed a penchant for lifting even lighthearted conversations to provocative reflections about salvation and matters of final consequence, and he did so with unassuming humility. This disposition provided a good check and balance on my rather petulant, raw and more secular style. Even though filtered through the screens of Christianity, I retained from my Worcester Avenue days a goodly amount of unsocialized brashness.

Ethan's world was one of convincing and totalizing faith, authenticated by non-pretentious holiness. His lifestyle was discernibly near to what the Bible instructed, natural, easy and integrated, never as a matter of course. He endearingly reminds me of those we serve in West Africa. There, the unexpected stranger or anxiously awaited arrival of a relative or guest is not a social inconvenience, but something to be instantly and continuously celebrated. Taking care of the elderly in the most sacred and respectful manner, providing tender care for children, and compassionately responding to the plight of the poor, the hurting, and the outcast is intrinsic to their worldview. The notion that God does not, or may not, exist is not even thinkable. They worship God whether the rains pour or whether the sun shines. Their collective cultural and religious résumé was Ethan's personal one, almost construct by construct.

Ethan was pre-cut for the clergy. By all indices of religious "callings," his was unequivocal, was from God, and was one he lived every day of his life reckoning with. It is inconceivable to ever view him separate from a defensibly clear relationship to ministry. In what is commonly referred to as a "trial sermon" in the African American church, his was from the Book of Isaiah, the sixth chapter. Seeking a readied candidate to bring a message to His people, God asked, "Whom can I send? Who will go for us?" Isaiah's and Ethan's response was, ". . . here am I, Lord, send me . . ."

Ethan was not unlike prophets and apostles from the Hebrew and New Testament Scriptures who, when a poignant voice of hope was needed, they answered the call. He was not a flashy, flamboyant or a power-wielding person; nor did he fare comfortably well with most of his fellow clergy who were, perhaps especially not with them. He never sought to be in the glare of the public spotlight, but he was one of those, "let me lead by personal example," individuals who avoided outward displays of his religion.

His theology was active, real and alive, characterized by an unrehearsed dynamic that at times appeared to have preceded its principles and dogmas. He read the Bible and prayed each morning and evening, and without being pharisaic or condescending, he reminded those of us close to him to do the same. His faith constructions were all-encompassing, quite noticeably, with respect to "women in the pulpit" discussions of that day, he was a proponent of gender inclusion. Some of his minister friends actually stopped having fellowship with him because he ordained women and had them actively preaching in his church. This forgivingly pained him.

Ethan was particularly fond of the theology of Geraldine Peterkin, a charismatic woman whose roots were in the Methodist church. Sister Pete, as her followers affectionately called her, established interdenominational prayer groups throughout the city. Her weekly gatherings alternated in followers' homes, and they were especially attractive to blacks frustrated with inertia in the established church. Ethan was drawn to Sister Pete's non-dogmatic approach to faith and her views on diversity. He credited his introduction to the "spirit-filled life" to her, and he frequently referenced his spiritual understanding, advocacy, and affirmation of women in the ministry to her teachings.

With a ministerial career that spans more than forty years, it would not be an exaggeration to suggest that during that time he personally did as much for the Pittsfield community as anyone in its history—clergy, civic, and social leaders included. He moved with celestial reverence to and from different denominationally, socially and racially segregated neighborhoods, more often than not, suspending his own schedule of priorities to do so.

Ethan never failed to seize an opportunity to tend to the pain of the bruised, those close to him, and those who weren't. I vividly recall a Pittsfield minister calling me one Sunday afternoon to reprimand me for an infraction I had committed against one of his children. Extremely vulnerable and disjoined, I sought counsel from Ethan. He provided me a paradigm of accountable healing that soothed the ache in my soul, but he did so without alienating himself from this minister with whom he was also a friend. He had this marvelous knack for integrated ministering, coupled with non-discriminatory theology.

Ethan developed a reputation around the city of being a person who could be consistently counted on to visit the sick, be there for anxious prison inmates, feed the hungry, irrespective of color or creed, and make as many house calls as necessary when domestic squabbles warranted his counsel. The voluminous portfolio of these initiatives came as a direct response to his understanding of Christian theology. He always referenced Jesus as his motivation for action, minus the annoyance of self-righteousness that some include when doing so. He acted without ulterior motives when performing deeds of goodness, and he graciously poured out his life to help fill theirs when they were doing badly. His was a relentless journey of mending human suffering, because for him it was the only theological option available.

Unlike intervention practices that are short lived, politically motivated and opportunistic, he visibly followed paths of pain until there were clear signs of relief. He insisted on tracking people whose rocky roads he felt privileged to cross—I want to say, driven to stay with their course. He couldn't rest until he knew how the forgotten, exploited, and bruised were doing. As he moved in and out of their lives with affirming love, they had the comforting feeling that they were his friends—in a large number of cases, each of them thought they were his best friend. They were—all countless numbers of them.

Ethan found time to frequently visit nearly every African American church in the city, and some white ones. He spent a lot of time in Pentecostal and Charismatic communities of faith, even those that found and publicly proclaimed his Baptist theology inferior to theirs. But he didn't let their views affect his Christian concept of love and tolerance, clearly not forgiveness. To him, those who didn't agree with his beliefs were brothers and sisters in Christ, case closed.

Providing no shortage of pastoral leadership in his own church, as he viewed it, his calendar was filled with the anniversaries, ordination services, baptisms, programs and assorted services of his friends. He didn't attend the myriad activities to have his presence publicly noted; he did so because he genuinely believed in supporting his friends, deriving righteous pleasure from just being in their company.

Reconciling growth-inhibiting differences and building bridges to groups living on different sides of the track launched Ethan onto other stages of engagement. He was a member of the NAACP, worked in a number of grass roots' organizations, and selectively entered those arenas where he thought he could make a difference in caring for one more child, in housing one more of the homeless, and in turning one more addict away from drugs. He was never confused about which had primacy, as he moved between social, civic, and religious theaters. He was first and foremost a Christian, then a minister, following the life and teachings of Jesus even when others refused or defected. In the 1960s, for example, it became fashionable for young African Americans to target the church as a source of resentment and hostility: not Ethan. He held on to his faith, was, in fact, more of an apologist for its credibility then than at any other time.

4
Joined at the Hip

The exact occasion on which Ethan and I met is a little vague to me, probably at some gospel singing or preaching event. I do know that I had begun to move around Pittsfield with as much diligence on the religious circuit as I had previously done on "the avenue," making it inevitable that we would meet.

Neither of us carried the burden of gender conflict or cross over in our long acquaintance—we weren't gay. Two African American male friends of more than thirty-five years, we had a deep and sacred love for each other, articulated in a relationship that inexorably drove us to our respective celebrations, hard times and pains. Popular mythology that minimizes such rooted connections between black men, or that fails to highlight their presence in discussions on the subject, was sufficiently negated in ours. We enjoyed an incredibly rich fraternity, not unlike those entrancing bonds more readily portrayed in African American women's *Sistah to Sistah* stories.

Ethan and I didn't have the benefit of rituals to delineate our friendship, unbridled by time and situation. We were brothers without the frills, even culturally popular and prescribed ones. We also didn't need commercial hypes, ". . . I love you man . . . " lead-ins to legitimate us. By definition of how we understood our relationship, we could always be found acting in ways that viewed the interests of "the other" as more important than those of "the I."

We forged an indissoluble tandem of fraternal and theological unity. I tried being there for him, to walk with him on his roads of joy and humiliation, the latter being the longest, with ". . . many a winding turn . . ." and to help negotiate his decades of troubles, heartaches, and reverses.

Clearly, I was the more likely beneficiary in the relationship. I made no achievement nor incurred any failure in which he wasn't near. He attended all my graduations, from Chicago and Greenville, Illinois, to New York City and New Brunswick, New Jersey. When I was burned in an incinerator fire in Brooklyn one day, he dropped everything and drove four hundred miles to visit me. He flew to Massachusetts to participate in my installation at Boston University, School of Theology. He accompanied me to a high school reunion because I was nervous about going alone, and he joined me at grave ceremonies when burying my family's dead. He came to Africa to see evidence of some intercontinental visioning that we had done together as teenagers, and he would later express interest in coming there to work with me.

The last public act he did on my behalf was a few years prior to his death. Because it positioned him in his typical role of bailing out his friends, and because it represented so much of what we had labored hard over the years to address—regressive ecclesiastical behavior—it is one whose details are worth repeating. When I couldn't return to my home church, St. James, to conduct a ceremony of thanks for the contributions its living and deceased members had made on my life, Ethan granted those I wanted to acknowledge asylum in his church, Mt. Holly.

In denying me the thanks' opportunity, St. James's pastor indicated that he didn't want to set a precedent for others seeking to make similar coming home requests. How curious, Ethan and I commiserated. When Jesus questioned the one returning leper of the whereabouts of the other nine thankless ones, He seemed to be stressing the value of remembering, of expressing gratitude as a morally important act. When I returned to thank my home church, its pastor said that that was precisely what he didn't want. Hmmm!

Never mind the fact that I grew up in St. James, and that my mother has been one of its staunchest members for more than fifty years, which, of course, entitle neither of us to anything. However, my request was not an attempt to pull rank nor did it hinge on entitlement: It was spiritual, conceived in the deepest parts of the church's belly, the place from which I acquired unforgettable lessons on faith. If the harbingers of this once nurturing cradle of righteousness could have been made aware of this no-thanks policy, they would turn over in their graves. Maybe the angels of record keeping will deliver a copy of its text to their coffin doors, and they will return in thundering garments of glory to inquire what is going on in the place they left in our charge.

If the notion is true that you can always go home to family, it wasn't true for me that you can always go home to church—not even to your home church. The thought of not being allowed to return to the religious house in which I grew up, to not walk the spiritual aisles where its pioneering mothers and fathers walked, to not be able to look over at the choir pews where I once sang, or to kneel at the altar where its venerable saints included my name when they prayed, nor break bread and drink from the communion cup at my home church was just heartbreaking.

It was just heartbreaking.

Youth Crusaders for Christ

One of the signatures Ethan and I put in the city's religious story was the conception of *Youth Crusaders for Christ* (YCC), an organization in which a loose aggregation of Pittsfield's black youth decided to be a more focused and directed one. We conducted local youth meetings, revivals and programs, and made several evangelism runs out of state, in pursuit of making our mark on the black church, and introducing spiritual renewal chartered by young people of destiny. Ethan was our spiritual leader; he scrutinized who should be in the group and set the tone for its theological parameters. I was the group's strategist and worked hand and in hand with him, as did Lawrence Flemming, its tactician. Joseph Lowe was male soloist and Reuben Skipow, a twelve-year-old musical phoneme, its pianist/organist.

Reuben couldn't technically read music, but he could play perfectly any rendition after hearing it once, instantly integrating his own improvisational inserts for appeal. He revolutionized the way the organ was played in black gospel in western Pennsylvania and beyond.

Marti Wright was YCC's female vocalist. She personally brought more class to the group than the rest of us did in combination, lifting expectant audiences to euphoric heights when she sang. She was an unrivalled talent, who would later go on to succeed in Hollywood as a performing and recording artist. Just as Ethan had died years later when I was in Africa, she had died years earlier when I was there. Not many days pass without our thinking of her, and missing her even more.

YCC'ers were theologically daring and untamed, believing that we could do anything. We viewed the faith journey as an awfully serious undertaking but were not narcissistic, fascinated with the aromas of our own church affiliations. Instead, we sought the larger trans-dogma connections, which freed us and freed us more. Unfortunately, with the passage of time, some of our associates retreated to the kind of narrow theological thinking that we had worked so fastidiously hard to avoid when younger—the kind that gave us distinction and cross-denominational acceptance.

My pastor, Rev. Shils, opened up the doors of St. James for YCC's rallies, as did his successor, Rev. William Dothan. Both had a genuine compassion for the development of young people. The St. James on their watch was clearly different from the one I unsuccessfully sought to return to say thanks.

In preparation for YCC convocations, nailing up posters, passing out flyers, and having planning sessions throughout the city was important, in terms of our goal of engagement. But the meetings, as we generically referred to them, were the focus. The guys all wore "blue Danube" shirts, starched and pressed so stiff that they would stand up on their own. Marti wore a matching blue blouse. We sported identical white ties and routinely poured about a gallon of English Leather and Old Spice on us, climaxing the preparation ceremonies by soaking our underarms with five-day deodorant pads. I get the "heebie-jeebies" just thinking about it. I suspect if I came anywhere near these products now, my flesh would go into hives, or shock, or something.

And then there were those always dreaded moments when Ethan put on Magic Shave. This is a shaving powder that requires no razor for removing stubborn facial hair, with a smell that would so repulsively scent the house that pets would rush out the back door—competing with us for exit priority. The antidote to this Magic Shave inhibitor was the sweet fragrance of Marti. Whatever she sprayed on made us feel as though we were walking past the women's cologne section in Saks Fifth Avenue. She was a spring rose whose very presence sweetened the air around her that we breathed. Many a day Ethan, and his bad-smelling shaving powder, escaped our wrath because Marti was around.

Make no mistake; all this body adornment stuff was secondary to our more serious business, the proclamation of the *good news*. Ethan made sure of that. YCC meetings brought participants from all over the greater metropolitan area. Baptists and Methodists, Lutherans and Presbyterians, members of Churches of God in Christ, Churches of God and Apostolic faiths all courageously helped us to reverse, theretofore, segregated worship. We were instrumental in getting singers to sing, liturgists to conduct worship, intercessors to pray and preachers to preach *in their own tongue*, legitimating the feeling that inter-denominational expressions of faith, in the same place and at the same time, was more than a notion. It was happening right before our eyes.

One of the things that kept us sane and on track was our ability to laugh; we could, and did, find something funny in everything. When Reverend Farr's prayer went on a bit too long at a St. James's rally, as an example, one of us would be called upon to stop him, somehow, some way; just stop him. With guests in the church and a revival service to get underway, we knew that we couldn't let our senior brother pray on into the 15-minute frame. The dye fell my way. I quietly eased down out of my chair, crawled on my hands and feet, face up, and gave Reverend Farrell a shoe to shoe jolting kick. His Amen suddenly came to a welcomed end, though the snickering in back of me stayed throughout the service, actually for years to come, now that I think of it.

Then there was the time we went to Bluefield, West Virginia to conduct a crusade and Ethan forgot his insulin and shoes. For the insulin, no problem: we got that from the local pharmacist. The shoes, however, was a different matter. Since all of ours were too big for him, we had to camouflage his feet in sneakers, carefully draping his pants over them. We could only hope that he wouldn't get an unusual burst of preaching energy and jump pulpit height. Come as you are and wear what you want was unthinkable then, particularly sporting tennis shoes in the pulpit—for whatever reason. Ethan was contained while preaching and kept both feet floor level, though we laughed far into the night afterwards.

While evangelism in and out of Pittsfield was immeasurably valuable to us, the many families in whose homes we frequently went provided us the real fellowship deal. When not at the Goldens eating and whooping it up, we could be found at the Turners, Goodens, and Blockers, with an occasional drop in at the Wrights and Floyds. Most important in these extended family connections was the Lam family, Ethan's parents, in particular. We were adopted in the Lam home as our home away from home. It was our theological and social sanctuary, whether at the dinner table, in the living room or in the upstairs bedrooms where often we all piled into a couple of beds and talked, and joked all night.

Ethan's mother, "Mother Lam," always prepared for 3 or 4 extra mouths to feed, especially on Sunday afternoons. I invariably tried my best to be one of those getting to the table first, pushing and pulling if necessary. Without a doubt, she prepared the best green beans, cornbread, fried chicken, and potato pies in town. I make an effort to get by there whenever I'm in Pittsfield for a little eating nostalgia, a little (over) indulgence if you please.

Deacon Lam, Ethan's father, regarded us as his children. He never gave preferential treatment to his blood offspring, but he judiciously divided his love among us all. His well-known teary conversations about faith matters served as inspiring motivation when we were down or indecisive. And because we didn't always fit comfortably within conventional ecclesiastical worlds, that was often. He was that still water that ran deep, with and for us.

In a conversation I had with one of his grandsons on the historic relevance of the African American church, about which he was skeptical, I made reference to his grandfather,

Deacon Lam. I reminded him that he was a born and bred member of that church and was one of the most genuine Christians I had ever met. I told him that he could always be found at the bedside of a sick patient, on the doorstep of a hungry family with a bag of groceries or sharing the gospel with the lonely. I told him how inspiring things got at the "mourners bench" when his grandfather sang those old call-to-worship Baptist hymns.

When deacon and Mother Lam would retire and leave the downstairs to us on Sunday nights, we sprawled out on the floor, taught and learned from each other our greatest instruction on theology. Topics on why it was important to avoid doctrinal dogmatism, how to maintain apostolic integrity in a climate of theological and cultural apostasy, and why we should sustain our Christian commitments, despite the appealing attractions wooing us to drift, kept us busy. None of my institutional training on these subjects was as comprehensive as these spontaneous seminars at the Lam's.

I have often thought about these days, when just a few years prior, a few blocks away in the basement of Mike Smith on Rhine Avenue, I was involved in a wholly different kind of venture. There, we used to play cards for hours. I recall how we viciously ripped into our knuckles in a card game bearing the same name, where drawing blood for winners provided a sense of ultimate triumph, for losers, pain and agony.

Sunday evenings at the Lam's were refreshingly different, listening to 33LP recorded sermons of Rev. C. L. Franklin, and the broadcasts of C.M. Ward, Billy Graham, G.A. Humph, and the melodious homiletics of Eugene Ward. When these programs signed off, on would go the record player with music from a succession of gospel singers, Mahalia Jackson, young Aretha Franklin, The Roberta Martin

Singers, The Pilgrim Travelers, The Clara Ward Singers, and, yes, the Caravans and James Cleveland.

In the mid-60s, Ethan and I determined that we needed to upgrade our levels of theological education. We began taking night courses at the Pittsfield Bible Institute, which after doing for a year or so, I applied to Mizpah Bible Institute in Chicago and convinced him to do the same. We knew that if Mizpah accepted us, we would have to leave our families and the YCC initiatives. Even though he hadn't long acquired a license for barbering, he would have to sever himself from that, as I would need to drop all my little odds and ends' jobs. More upsetting than anything for me was the fact that I would have to separate from Marti, for whom I had long-term plans.

The news came. We were admitted to Mizpah, the "West Point of Christian education." We were off to the big city, Chicago! We sort of felt like that first-time visitor to New York in one of Stevie Wonder's recordings, who, after disembarking at Port Authority Bus Terminal, looked up on Eighth Avenue and said, ". . . New York! Just like I pictured it, . . . skyscrapers, *everthang . . .* " In our case, it was Chicago, just like we pictured it, though we ended up dramatically different from the newcomer to New York in Stevie's song. He ended up in jail for being in the wrong place at the wrong time. We would have our lives transformed for being in the right place at the right time. Visiting the jailed, in fact, would become an integral part of our life's work.

We were overwhelmed with Chicago's sheer size and magnificent architecture. More than the largest city we have ever seen, housing the tallest buildings and metropolitan complexity we had ever witnessed, it was the place we had prayed hard and fervently about going to, the place we hoped would satisfy our insatiable appetite for biblical knowledge.

I went to day school and Ethan enrolled for evening classes, a dual track that gave us the best opportunity for optimally acquiring the fullest possible range of information. The rigors of our study routines and staying in different locations didn't allow us to visit with each other during the week. He stayed with his sister not too far away from the Institute, and I lived on campus. We made it a point, however, to talk regularly about our new challenges, about the diverse culture of the city, and generally continued providing mutual support, *vis a vis* our bond in righteousness—as had been the case in Pittsfield.

The school's instructional intensity and demanding regimen brought us some much-needed discipline; we would never approach biblical scholarship and ministry the same. Ethan and I were especially attracted to the Institute's Practical Christian Work Assignments, PCWs. These were "hands on" activities designed to expose students to culturally sensitive opportunities in which to do ministry, though there was a race based difference in the structure of these opportunities. In white communities, the learning and tutoring mission reinforced presumed literacy on salvation matters. In those with peoples of color, the objective was more explicitly evangelical, to introduce clearer, if not truer, understandings of theology.

My first placement was at Sister Miller's on the South Side. Ethan's was at Pastor Rain's church, a white Southern Baptist minister sent to Chicago to provide a ministry for urban blacks, also on the South Side. Pastor Rain talked slow and monotonic, and he would invariably put me to sleep when preaching. But he and his family were some of the nicest and most genuine people we met in the Mizpah experience. They loved the Lord and those to whom they were sent to minister.

Ethan's reverential ways were as winsome in Chicago and at Pastor's Rain's church as they had been in Pittsfield. Everyone liked him and recognized that his life and ministry were exemplary. Even though he and I regularly sought refuge in black churches Sunday evenings, Ethan never failed to be at pastor Rain's on Sunday mornings, graciously using his gifts and skills to teach, preach, and enrich the lives of those in that fellowship.

My second assignment was at Chicago's famous Pacific Garden Mission, a downtown rescue center where a gospel message was nightly preached, a hot meal provided, and clothing distributed to some of the city's most needy. Because of his eagerness to learn as much as he could, Ethan often joined me. Pacific Garden brought us eye to eye with " . . . the least of these, my brethren . . . " whom we believe Jesus had reference to in Matthew's gospel, chapter 25.

Other PCW placements introduced us to ministry with children and youth in ways we had not been privileged to embrace, as well as to international theology. As Mizpah impacted my commitment to later work in Africa, it provided the impetus for Ethan's leadership with some children at the Anna Park Housing Development, a residential area for some of Pittsfield's economically poor families.

When not fulfilling PCW assignments, class and related matters, we busied ourselves with other things, "Operation Wells Street," being one. This was a project I proposed to the Mizpah family a year after being there. Its objective was to bring attention to the plight of indigent people living directly in back of the school, those whom students felt theologically called to give gospel tracts and spiritual messages to, but more reluctant to impact their social needs.

I solicited members of the MBI family to bring usable but good clothing to these neighbors when returning from an Easter recess. The response was great. They brought nearly a ton of clean, wearable things to our neighboring friends. This effort helped us put flesh and bones, not just soul and spirit, on those who theretofore, had been mere numerical subjects of statistical evangelism.

The invisible walls between the Institute and their back-door neighbors weren't the only ones with which to be reckoned. There were a few within its sacred corridors, the ominous presence of racial disparity.

Racial unawareness in white evangelical communities typically includes phobic reactions associated with interracial dating, something assumed to be the motives of black males too socially friendly with white females. While Ethan and I had no intentions of bringing white brides back to Pittsfield, we thought it best to seek refuge in African American homes and churches whenever possible—familiar places to raise our voices, to clap our hands and pat our feet, and to fraternize with the *sisters*.

The idea of having to constantly differentiate between prejudice-free expressions of acceptance, and those that intuitively and obviously weren't, was something we had not anticipated. We hadn't come to Chicago to rectify deviations from biblical and constitutional instruction on racial equality, and our own history replete with their demonstrated violations. We had come to study. But whether we liked it or not, this was our situation, and it wasn't an easy ride. Boarding that bumpy shuttle that took us from affirming African American environments, to "on trial until further notice" in white ones, was draining. It is an experience that most white evangelicals know nothing about. They have no frame of reference to understand those sitting next to them in church services singing "Great Is Thy Faithfulness"—is often, for them, a perpetual treadmill of anguish.

When white students came to the Institute, they had few such cognitive adjustments to make. Theirs was a natural transition from, say, the average Southern Baptist church in Silver Spring, Texas, to Elm Street Evangelical Church on the North Side of Chicago. While the big city might have been more than expected for some of them, they didn't have the burden of tradition and history—weighted with race and ethnic bias—to overcome.

Against the backdrop of this enigma, to repeat, Ethan and I stayed within close proximity of our theological and cultural heritage, a heritage we knew had *"brought us thus far, along the way."* We stretched ourselves over Chicago's African American denominational mix whenever we could. Our goal hadn't changed: It was to develop doctrinally sensitive, integrated and inclusive views on practical theology with sound biblical teaching. Chicago's rich social and religious diversities helped provide the former, Mizpah, the latter.

When not actively engaged in matters connected to the Institute family, and when not within fellowship reach of the African American church, we spent time—unforgettable time—with our new Windy City friends. Just as God had given us loving families in whose homes we enjoyed unconditional acceptance in Pittsfield, He did so in Chicago. He gave us the Reids, Rains, Andrews, and Millets. He gave us Ethan's Aunt Martha and Uncle Evers. He gave us Sister Aigens, who could always be counted on to make sure we had a good home-cooked meal, especially on Sundays and holidays. I used to eat so much of her food that I had to walk sideways into the "L" train when returning to the Institute.

These Chicago friends were our family in the truest sense of African and African American familism, not to mention the fact that they were affirming followers of Jesus. Ethan and I would never think of Mizpah and Chicago, and the enormous impact both had on our lives, without noting their loving presence.

5

Ethan Gets Married

Ethan met a young lady whom he was intent on marrying. The early report was that she had taught him how to play tennis and had kissed him, probably his first kiss. She was also a professing Christian. While not necessarily the checklist he might have sought under different circumstances, he was charmed. He was in love. The news of all this sent shock waves throughout Pittsfield because everyone had expected him to ask Mrs. Bleekers's daughter, Patricia, to be his wife. That familiar theme, boy or girl leaves home for school or the military, and returns with an unexpected marriage plan, had become Ethan's. He would bring his bride home, not get her from there: "Look y'all, guess who's coming home . . . as my wife?"

Some of us were not altogether settled with his plans, but we piled into our cars and went off to Chicago for the big event. Ethan had provided all the theologically and socially correct answers to our questions about the marriage, and we accepted them. He was our senior brother and we—well, we just accepted them.

Theirs was a double wedding ceremony, held at Beritan Baptist Church and officiated by a close friend of Ethan's fiancé. Ethan would later convey serious reservations concerning this minister, with respect to his indiscreet entrance into their marriage covenant. The ceremonies lasted forty-five minutes, after which the wedding parties motored off to the reception.

I was in the car with Ethan's father, convoying directly behind Ethan and his bride. Not long en route, we were a bit puzzled, because they weren't talking or looking at each other, the way you'd expect two people who had pledged themselves to a forever covenant together less than an hour earlier. He was driving, while she was sitting at the extreme right of the car, listlessly gazing out of the passenger window. I dismissed the idea of compelling scenic surroundings as distractions; I also knew that the car, like all "back in the day" cars, had no front seat consul to so physically distance them from each other. Sisters sitting on the passenger side could move as close as they wanted to the brothers, and they usually did. As soon as the old Packard had backed out of the driveway, and was out of viewing range of curious parents, most of them nudged so close to the brothers that you would have thought they were posing for a penny-arcade photo on a stool, one stool. No, this nuptial scene wasn't a scenic distraction or seating problem. Whatever was happening, we could only hope that it was a case of temporary, post marital jitters and not a sign of things to come, that when well-wishers and supporters had gone their way, the Lams would pull it all together. Only time would tell.

The following day they packed their gifts and belongings and headed to Pittsfield, to set up shop, house and ministry.

Setting up shop meant that Ethan would return to barbering, in order to earn a living. Along with a partner, he opened the Hods-Lam Barber Shop on Worcester. He also invested in a laundromat a few blocks away, as well as purchased a small income generating rooming house on Pittsfield's East Side. These initiatives showed his industry and determination to break the cycle of being a user of services. He was to be a producer of some. With a high school diploma, an honorable military discharge, and his Mizpah Evening School Bible training, he knew that he couldn't just sit around and wait for things to happen. He would need to be aggressively enterprising to support his family, to force the action on their behalf.

Working multiple jobs is still a harsh reality that many African American ministers have to deal with, contrary to the myth that they *all* live in palatial opulence and are materialistically overindulgent. Most have to work conventional employment in order to get medical insurance, sick pay, pension and retirement benefits.

The Lams opened house in Pittsfield, initially renting one across the street from Ethan's parents on Nat Street, later purchasing one on Dodge Avenue. They would give birth to two children, a boy and a girl. As the new Lam clan on the block, Ethan did the absolute best he could, all the technically, morally and theologically right things, to place them on the *good foot.* He continued copiously following the Bible for instructions on how he should conduct himself in his family, viewing his spiritual leadership as paramount. He applied the Scriptures' teachings on how Lam family members ought to behave before God, between each other and with outsiders. He daily prayed *for* them, and he instituted regular Bible study and prayer *with* them. Especially consistent at it when the children were young, he set aside a special time in the week to go out as a family, frequenting different restaurants, taking long car rides, and enjoying other wholesome recreational activities for family enrichment. He continued these outings with his daughter long after their meaning for the family, *qua* family, became moot.

Like many fathers—I guess it's *a man's thang*—Ethan wanted his son to follow in his footsteps, though to walk further and faster. He sent him to a private Christian academy for his primary education, and he proudly watched him become a standout leader in high school. This son would later also go to a Bible institute, but not guided by quite the same philosophic and theological ideas of his father. His views on the traditional African American community, for example, were a bit more tenuous than that of his father; but Ethan never let their differences affect his abiding readiness to provide his son care and support.

Ethan deeply cherished both their children, though gradually leaned in confidence and affection toward his daughter. She became the one in whom he would center his best aspirations, a position his son had similarly achieved in his wife's favor. Fittingly, when Mrs. Lam was in Chicago for the Christmas holidays in 1996, including that dismally dark day when the curtains precipitously closed on Ethan's life, his daughter was in the house. She prepared him his *last supper*, or final late morning meal, as the case was. While he literally died the following day in a local hospital, for all intents and purposes, he expired in her arms the day before, at home.

Ethan had a boundlessly feverish love for his wife, which compared to most men I knew was nothing short of human incomprehension. He was in his glory when she showed even the slightest signs of endearment towards him. Nothing pleased him more than taking advantage of those opportunities he had to showcase her as *madam,* and as mother of his children. Sometimes before preaching, he would speak of her sterling qualities from the pulpit, those he advertised to be real and those he imagined and projected. She was the wind underneath his sails.

His love for Mrs. Lam was like a huge covenant cloth, crocheted with tolerance and forgiveness, in accord with his perception of Christian spousal love. Though it was far from a perfect rendition, as most humanly constructed efforts are, he did his best to *make it real.* However, having had little experience on the practical side of love and romance, and being too stubborn or shy to ask, rumors leaked from Dodge

Street were that he was a bit mechanical, passionless and devoid of warm facilities of expression. Whatever inhibitions may have affected his ability to make love more identifiably affectionate, one thing was never in question: He adored and worshiped the ground on which his wife walked.

Ethan had no unreasonable expectations for her to augment the family income by working, even though for most of their marriage she had a part-time job at a local school. He didn't even seem to mind that she showed prima donna inclinations, special privileges, treatment and benefits inherently connected to traditional black ministers' wives, most notably identified in their "first lady" designations.

As long as Mrs. Lam was happy and attended the children, Ethan was content. Even though he appeared to be occasionally embarrassed when guests visited their home, regarding its upkeep, it was never a serious enough matter to prompt a domestic crisis. The truth is, Mrs. Lam could do little wrong. When there was the slightest indication that she might, the love he had for her was atoning-sufficient to prohibit any sustained criticism or correctives. Ethan construed his relationship with her in the exact biblical way that Christ as bridegroom is portrayed with the church, His bride. Both, wives to natural husbands, and the church to Jesus, are cast in the redemptive position of being loved despite their imperfections, of having their bridegrooms sacrifice their lives in the face of persisting contradictions, ingratitude, recalcitrance, and rebellion.

Later, when the storms began blowing over the Lam marriage, threatening its covenant restraints, opportunities, and liberties, Ethan found meaning precisely in what he perceived to be its divine, eternal purpose. As an institution, in this sense, his marriage could not be legitimately questioned, invalidated nor tampered with by others—not even, especially, should I say, by himself or his wife. He was to be a husband to one wife and father to her children only, to love and care for them until death, *c'est tous*.

With the same certainty that we, his closest friends, would cage ourselves with deadly beasts, believing in his virginity before marriage, we will do so regarding his unerring fidelity during it. Ethan never betrayed the moral covenant interdicting an extra-marital affair. While we didn't strap ankle bracelets on him to telegraph his behavior and whereabouts twenty-fours a day, there is no evidence that he ever, ever made an advance toward another woman during the more than thirty years he was married. There is none that he has ever even kissed one, albeit, social and religious cheek greetings. He shared with me incidences in which overtures were made at him, but ones that he summarily dismissed, on occasion having to leave his Bible and counseling manuals on the dining room table on the way out. The imagery of the Old Testament's Joseph, last seen running through the door out of the outstretched arms of Potiphar's wife, might best describe him during these encounters.

6

Pastoring: from Trial to Tribulation, to Tribulation

Setting up shop and house in Pittsfield was ancillary to Ethan's larger vision. Always in the background of his every waking moment was some sort of theological work.

Significantly more than formal posts, on which he would embark, Ethan wanted to closely mimic the life of Jesus in his ministry, for his public life to be theologically inseparable from his private life. His was an everyday exercise of faith, in contrast to its special day of the week, episodic or situational versions. His aspiration to pastor was in concert with what he understood the Bible to mean for this office, something that was apparent in his conversations, in his un-staged visits to places inhabited by the hurting and in his benevolence to the needy. Ironically, this intentional integration of Christian values and life practice would end up in places not prepared for their embodiment, in churches. What he didn't realize was that adhering to the teachings of the Bible might be occupationally hazardous when doing so in places expressly established for their presence.

The African American church is an unblended mixture of the greatest and the least in us; the greatest because it has always been reliably near to guide us through some of our darkest hours—the least, because it could do incredibly more than that. Having an obtrusive theology that catapults "darkest hours" to the forefront of its liturgy and preachments, it appears to have as many issues with its collective self-image as some of its members have with their individual ones.

This conflict places African-American pastors in a dubious position, requiring them to do much more than preach and pray; they are given the therapeutic task of fixing altered self-concepts, those of their congregations as well as their own. Pastors unable to make the grade will often tender their homiletics in the vernacular of the streets—trashing, dumping, and beating congregates into polemic and symbolic submission, accenting their already fragile constructions of self-esteem. Others work more conscientiously at rehabilitating this damage, while still others manipulate it for profit—psychologically and monetarily. Upper echelon ministers will often wear the best-looking clothing, spray on the sweetest smelling perfumes, drive the finest cars, and live in the most luxurious homes to compensate for these image deficits.

As for their members, no matter how economically poor they are, they will cough up large bucks to be conferred cascading levels of meaning and affirmation. They will award pastors who give them sufficient amounts a wide array of gifts, *may* even *travel from the east to bring frankincense, gold, and myrrh to lay at their cribs.* At its basest level, they will transfer the lack of their own personal fulfillment back onto pastors, if necessary, begging, borrowing and bartering it for them. They care little that they have standards of living far above theirs; really, they wouldn't have it any other way. For, in them, their ministers, they see *themselves* all fancied up—from home, to garage, to jewelry, to clothing, to vacation spots. Let's call it, "image enhancement transference."

One of the ways this phenomenon manifests itself in everyday church life is similar to the "keeping up with the Jones" syndrome, whereby pastors and church members are forever in pursuit of bragging rights on who has the best ecclesiastical deal in town. They expend a goodly amount of time comparing edifices, membership statistics, number of

Sunday morning services, baptism candidates' count, and educational levels of their constituencies. Bigger church leaders and members more freely cite their Sunday offerings in casual, though quite intentional, conversations with their colleagues; the more that pastors say they take in, the more they want to be viewed as top or up and coming top brass. You can peek in on all this, say, at church conventions. When pretending to read a book at the vendor's booth, you can hear their tediously boring conversations on "church growth, small talk" in the next booth. That would be the booth on the other side of the one selling videos on successful "hooping," which is next to the one selling tapes on how to speak in tongues, next to the one selling step by step graphics on how to shout.

This business of church image and status is part of the latent background against which Ethan's checkered journey in the pastorate would take, a journey that would eventually lead him to an un-welcomed appointment that cold December day in 1966, when the sun refused to shine and the stars wouldn't come out at night.

Ministering at Anna Park, Coply Street, Shilah, and Mt. Holly

Ethan's first assignment was a voluntary one on Pittsfield's north side, the Anna Park Housing Development. Every Sunday morning he faithfully went to serve the needs of this community's un-churched, abandoned and, sometimes, unloved children. To watch him teach and sing, something he couldn't do in tune if his life depended on it, and love these children into the kingdom, was a *sweet savor unto God.* Just the idea that a "homeboy" had gone off to distant Chicago to school and returned to share his life and knowledge was an inspiration to Anna Park residents.

His work at Anna Park, however, wasn't so viewed by many of the city's black clergy. This was a group that wouldn't work in these fields of service if their lives depended on it, would leave their motor running when popping in for a token hello. They viewed Anna Park as painfully unfulfilling, and as a place for clergy rejects, failures, and those biding their time for greater things—sort of like Methodist ministers being shipped off to Africa as theological punishment or "fine tuning" for bigger and better things.

As church members are known to "talk bad" about each other, so do ministers—about each other and their members. Ethan was the topic of their gibberish gab, exiled into insignificance *down there in those projects*, they whispered. Viable ministry for them was "hooping" through high tech microphone systems to churches packed with comfortably seated attendants, those ready to say Amen, clap and raise their hands to every preached phrase. But to Ethan, Anna Park was penultimate religious joy, an apostolic example of what Jesus called his followers to do.

His next three assignments were in organized churches, the big leagues. Here he would do combat with hardened, intransigent religious types, whose training by-passed classes on humility and cooperation. You would rather sleep in a hollow log and drink muddy water at a garbage land fill than be locked in battle with them. Ethan was wholly unprepared for the warfare they would wage and would come to quickly understand that molding the minds of innocent, disengaged children was one thing: re-molding the minds of religious adults was an entirely different matter.

His first traditional pastorate was at Coply Street Church of God. This was a holiness community that wasn't as provincially doctrinaire as were others in the city, those that scoffed at virtually all churches out of the charismatic, Pentecostal

and holiness loop. Coply Street and Ethan had been in court-
ship for some time, including his preaching regularly at their
Sunday evening fellowships. When its pulpit became vacant,
and after intensive deliberations on Ethan's candidacy, they
called him to be their pastor.

But it wasn't long before one of the church's most in-
fluential trustees, a man who had been an ardent fan of
Ethan's preaching ability and graceful approach in ministry,
began lobbying for his dismissal. Though no specific identification was given to the source of the tension, it was apparent that it was more than a passing scuffle.

Ethan was the model citizen, in terms of being a likable
and an impeccably righteousness person, but he lacked the
skills needed to govern the administrative side of church
development. And of course, the first thing you learn in
pastoral ministry, Course 101, is the necessity of having pol-
ished administration skills. Moral decency, righteous leadership, and having a vision for the alienated is secondary, and
rarely are the qualities of sainthood and management-wiz-
ardry found in one and the same person. They weren't
found in Ethan; he was soft, desired to keep peace at all
cost, and was repulsed by the slightest signs of conflict. He
had been in a small family-run church most of his life, and
he had absolutely no orientation for handling stubborn deacon and trustee boards and "point" men and women in
whose favor he might not find himself.

What those at Coply surprisingly discovered was that
Ethan's gentleness wasn't to be confused with him being a
pushover; that all that had to be done to bring him to the
dance was to change the music. Actually, each of his church
employers would make this discovery. The music would stop
and the dance at Coply was soon over, so to speak. Mutually
consented to by the church and Ethan, he would leave.

While Coply didn't exactly shower him with gifts of appreciation when the papers of separation were served, it was essentially an uneventful happening. No mud was slung at his car nor did he peel rubber in his old Studerbaker when exiting the parking lot.

Looking back at this relationship more reflectively, it may have been asking a little much for a conventional holiness church to wed a pastor from the Baptist persuasion, one not reared and doctrinally groomed behind its denominational walls. To its credit, Coply should probably be commended for even making the attempt.

Ethan then migrated to his Baptist roots and accepted a pastorate at Shilah Baptist Church, outside of Youngstown, Ohio. Since he really hadn't had a chance to put his vision and training into practice at Coply Street, this appointment would presumably be a good test for him and his ideas on evangelism and global missions, those honed in the Mizpah experience. Door-to-door canvassing, hospital and prison visitation, and identifying those in need in order to help them were some of the things he had in mind. He also thought that altering living options of the poor was within the reach of a progressive church ministry. On the matter of world missions, Ethan was a strong advocate of supporting missionaries, of them being budgeted a minimum of 10 percent from church offerings, and to have them regularly come to his church and talk about their work.

It all sounded so appealing during the honeymoon period of candidate preaching and the time immediately proceeding Ethan's installation—well, all but the proposal to give 10 percent church income to missionaries. The issue of money, and the way it's raised and distributed in black churches, is the *sine qua non* of its existence; global missions ranks nowhere near its center of importance.

In any case, this small eastern Ohio church was on the threshold of being launched into what it thought would be mainstream ecclesiastical engagement. It was the talk of the town. But a snag occurred, connected to the translation from Ethan's vision to its realization, essentially where the recruits were to come from who were to carry out the vision. When it was clear that they were to come from Shilah's membership—its boards, auxiliaries, and organizations—things weren't quite as rosy; they were so un-rosy that after two years, Shilah was ready to move on without Ethan as its pastor.

It would return to its tradition, "old-time hooping religion." The incompatible visioning, apparently undetected in the church's screening and interviewing procedures, as well as in Ethan's inability to get a good read, was the catalyst for the separation. I should also mention that the church was unable or unwilling to provide him a full-time salary, as it had promised to do. Neither he nor Shilah was satisfied with what they thought they had each contractually bargained for. They were history in each other's journey.

In a short period of time, Ethan had gone through two pastorates that hadn't worked out, and he was beginning to have self-doubts. At Coply it was a case of lacking administrative training and power-brokering skills. At Shilah it was case of trying to change ecclesiastical direction in old, anchored Baptist churches, which he learned was not easy and requires a measure of guile. But Ethan would have no part in anything that did not explicitly conform to his theology of love and grace; his style would remain conciliatory, accommodative, sympathetic, as would his mission to reach un-harvested domestic and global fields of opportunity.

With Coply and Shilah in back of him, Ethan began circulating his résumé to other churches around Pittsfield, including his home church, Mt. Holly Baptist Church. I encouraged him to seek a position in another city, suspecting that he needed a fresh and unfamiliar venue in which to do ministry. Having been a knee baby on the lap of his home church, I didn't feel he would get a fair shake, perhaps like that of Jesus, who despite his successes almost everywhere he went, his hometown residents couldn't get pass their conception that He was just a commoner. To them He was a mere "homey." Jesus became noticeably annoyed with their small-town pettiness and left, shaking off sandal dust in his trail. Whether Ethan would have to shake out street gravel from his loafer soles, when facing possible rejection, was the basis of my apprehensions.

Ministers being called to churches in which they grow up rarely works for either party, occasionally embroiling them in protracted bitterness, sometimes in embarrassing criminal proceedings. However, the call to Mt. Holly was too great for Ethan to resist. He would go there, toting his theological portfolio with him, the one he had taken on his previous assignments. His goals were the same as before, for the church to be more intentional in its evangelical thrusts and to embrace international missions.

Mt. Holly's goal was slightly different. It wanted to upgrade its own dossier, to give itself a face-lift. Having spent most of its religious life in a renovated garage in the lower bowels of the black community, it had physically moved to a new structure upon "Sugar Hill," and now wanted commensurate leadership. With the influx of young, articulate, and trained ministers filling African American pulpits around the city, Mt Holly wanted to be counted, seen and heard. What better way to do so than to have Ethan be their pastor, one of their own, one who would be sensitive to their history, idiosyncrasies, and needs.

With the death of its pastor, its son in the ministry was being called to move the church front and center, as a sort of "progressive-traditional" church, merging the new with the old. What neither Mt. Holly nor Ethan made clear was how this would impact their perspectives on church growth, and oversight that signaled danger. It was another situation where an overenthusiastic church and greatly excited candidate were inattentive to their respective underlying values, aspirations, and expectations. Its omission would prove to be disastrous this time, placing the church and Ethan on a path of calamitous confrontation.

The organizational apparatus for the conflict was a reactionary group of powerful church deacons and trustees, guardians of the vault housing church traditions and beliefs. Spearheaded by the chairman of the deacon board, this crafty bunch of pit veterans wedged a formidable alliance of division, destruction, and demonization that compares with guerrilla warfare.

For seven grueling years, they launched one of the most invidious and rancorous attacks against Ethan imaginable, shamelessly hurling unfounded and scurrilous fodder at him as an inadequate head of household and unfit pastor. It was a baseless scandal of incredible proportions, blighting the Pittsfield story like none other in its history. Not so much because it constituted an unforgivably disruptive intrusion into Ethan's journey, but because it had absolutely no grounding.

The most consequential was the embarrassment it brought to Ethan, personally. Moving around the city with invisible inscriptions of inadequacy and unfit sown on his lapel made him feel less than whole, if not unclean.

But the damage was also evident in the church, where there existed a systemic plan to undermine Ethan in virtually all of its business. One of the few times I was ever abrupt with Ethan was when over a two-year period he periodically asked me if Mt. Holly's secretary had forwarded a contribution to our work in Africa. I wasn't certain why he didn't know if she did or not, or if he was trying to save face because Mt. Holly hadn't really bought into his global missions' ideas. I later learned that the old head deacon, through whom all church disbursements had to be approved, refused to sign off on anything that did not reflect matters compatible with his church objectives, and was increasingly uncooperative regarding those Ethan wanted.

Then Ethan's preaching began taking a hit, and that's the last place black ministers want problems. Sunday mornings in the African American church, with the black preacher as centerfold, has traditionally been the highlight of the week, *for better or for worse, for richer or for poorer.* It's that time when pastors and members get ritually poised for celebration and those anxiously awaited spiritual opportunities immediately following the doxology the previous Sunday. If church members are not satisfied with the preachment component, it won't be long before the pastor's search committee is conducting secret meetings for his or her replacement, and not longer after that before they become public. One doesn't have to be the best preacher on the block—in the black church—but the congregation must perceive him to be. It may even accept the effort as simply going through the motions, but will send the minister packing if he doesn't turn some of the church water into wine as deserved compensation for mediocre and uninspiring preaching in its pulpit.

Not only was the quality of Ethan's preaching diminishing, his ability to cohere and energize the Sunday morning experience was. It was a cyclically interconnected decline, where the cause fed off of the effect and the effect the cause.

The weakening of his self-confidence was manifested in de-spirited worship, which in turn reflected poor preaching. On the one hand, he knew that when he stood at the podium he was preaching to people who were plotting his ouster—on the other, to those who might be their next recruits and allies. Once a gloriously moving experience, preaching had become a woefully lackluster chore for Ethan, a mere homiletic exercise that no longer complimented his calling. More than experiencing demoralization, he had become the embodiment of personal and liturgical malfunction, and was on weekly display as its validation.

To try and turn things around, he took the high road, where one assumes responsibility for wrongdoing whether guilty or not, and where what is of primary importance is reconciliation and harmony. But that didn't help. In pursuit of integrative resolution, Ethan tried another tactic. He called several meetings with church members, including with his primary accusers. He alternated different participant combinations—the entire congregation, one on one, one on three, officers and lay groupings, and the like. But he made little headway—little with Mt. Holly's rank and file, and, of course, less with its deacons and trustees.

Meanwhile, the alliance grew, much like an angry mob whose ill-conceived bantering attracts dissidents having no stake or reason in its cause. Ethan sought help outside the church, and he summonsed a diverse group of the city's clergy that were conversant with Baptist doctrine, as well as friends whose moral judgments and theology he trusted. When they met with the Mt. Holly alliance, they asked them to reveal the basis and nature of their malcontent. Barely audible, the head deacon said, ". . . Reverend Lam is aware . . . he is not the man of his house and is not the man of this church."

This was Ethan's and Mt. Holly's state of the union for months. Ethan showed signs of emotional and moral wear, and he polled his friends on what he should do. Some of them told him to "just hang in there," and that they were praying for him. Others, those from more activist theological persuasions, told him—in so many words—to pack up his books and Bibles and drop the keys to the church on the back pew when leaving. Of course, that was not an option, not because he hadn't had his fill, but because he believed that a way could be found to heal the relationship with Mt. Holly.

His saga worsened. He made the devastating discovery that his wife was in the fray, that she was integrally connected to Mt. Holly's rapacious initiatives to debunk him. She had the ear of the head deacon and was detailing a script of his supposed spousal inadequacy, his not being a "real man" and unable to meet her needs. It was rumored that she was having a hard time adjusting to the city, and that she wasn't happy with the slowness at which Ethan was acquiring things—more money, a bigger house, a prettier car and, well, more, bigger and prettier everything. But this "real man" talk was something quite different. It was a kind of betrayal not unlike that of a first century snitch that fingered an innocent Palestinian Jew named Jesus, a friend who co-sponsored the contract for his crucifixion.

With this revelation Ethan's bottom fell out. To whom could he now turn? He couldn't go to his church; its leaders were directing his chorus of humiliation. He couldn't turn to his friends; most of them could only tell him they were praying for him. He couldn't turn to his wife; she was on the take. All he could do was call on the name of the Lord, which he did. He did it, as we say, *way over in the mid-night hour.*

In his conundrum of hopelessness, I have likened Ethan to two characters in the Bible. The first is the Old Testament patriarch, Job, who was a victim of sudden family, property and personal loss, and anxiously looked everywhere for answers—to his friends, his wife, himself, and his God. His inquiry of anguish was essentially, "What have I done to deserve the situation in which I find myself?" The second is that of a rich man in the New Testament, a man who woke up one morning and discovered that he had a new residence, hell. In his state of burning torment, he couldn't get a drop of water to cool his scorching tongue, which like his entire being was on fire. Ethan's near panic-stricken search for answers to his moral and emotional dilemma, and his descent into hell's lower regions, also woke him up one day, alone, abused and in flames. As he moaned in drenching distress, there was no relief to be found. From those looking from without, and Ethan himself from within, the lines of his story are painfully close to Job's and those of the rich man.

More and more desperate, Ethan "silenced" the head deacon, a practice found, principally, in Pentecostal churches. Its latent function is to solidify discretionary pastoral power. Its official purpose is to punish church members for moral impropriety and incorrigibility. Whatever Ethan's motivation was, it was all but academic, because the deacon ignored the sanction. Instead of toning down his offensive, he tightened the noose around Ethan's neck, delightfully sniffing the stench of his flesh from the smoking cords. Pathologically obsessed to *take Ethan out*, the deacon was after a church hangin', he was. Nothing would quench his thirst for blood but the deafening cries of the crowd, the church crowd, "hang him," "hang him high."

It was a showdown at Mt. Holly's "O.K. Corral," one that stripped and left Ethan naked in the sanctuary of the congregation and bare in streets of the town, open places where he stood, powerless, beaten, and hurt. What began as a competitive quest for ecclesiastical parity, of "keeping up with the city's church Jones," and of bringing back the hometown kid to be its leading attraction, was now a brutal offensive to destroy him. Ethan was helpless and exposed—exposed for his innocence and holiness, while Mt. Holly seemed powerful, though also exposed. It was exposed for its guilt, moral indecency, and shame.

Many black Pittsfielders, who loved Ethan as much as they did any minister in the city, were shaken, like Rachael in Rama, *weeping and wailing for her children and refusing to be comforted* . . . This loud wailing was the cry of Bethlehem families whose innocent boy children, under the age of two, were sentenced to death by a ruthless king 2,000 years ago—an unimaginable noise of grief that ascended to heaven and descended to hell. Similarly, with the mutinous drama of betrayal and shame, unfolding at Mt. Holly, a spectacle of disgrace, the city's Hallelujah Chorus and song of joy were momentarily taken away, replaced by screeching hordes of demons gloating and chanting near their prey, Rev. Ethan Lam. Pittsfield women and men just couldn't understand what was happening to one of its favorite sons. There hadn't been any charges of fiscal irresponsibility; there was no report of an illicit affair; and he hadn't been negligent in his pastoral duties. What was it?

Ethan's life was now adrift. He no longer had a moral or theological mandate to continue his pastorate; he would soon be given an official vote for its discontinuation. As unchecked gangrene aggressively spreads in the body, the cancer of misery, rejection, and the senseless unknown was taking its toll on him, dangerously eating near his soul. The chasm between him and Mt. Holly grew wider and more furious, truly a tragedy in the absurd, one that would soon introduce him to his destiny with the hosts of heaven.

Rustling through the sordid lines of his story, I would embark on a campaign of determined inquiry to get some answers. A contentious church that pushed its pastor to the edge and a confused wife that pushed her husband over it wasn't enough for me. But what else was there? Was there some undisclosed meaning above and below Ethan's tale of woes, something indiscernibly tucked near the obvious that I could get at, perhaps?

I turned to a purely theological perspective, on the sovereignty of God and His incomprehensible doings in creation. I was tempted to conclude that the trials in Ethan's life were supposed to go as they had: that they were just supposed to. But this kind of speculation is never as satisfying as I would like, even though I accept its biblical presupposition. I embraced the synergistic idea that Ethan was destined to bear his crosses; but also that the elements causing suffering and pain in his life *require* clarity, cause and revelation. Theologically speaking, we know that Judas *had* to betray Jesus, but he paid a heavy price. It is not the purpose in this writing to address these age-old views on predestination and free will, least of all final judgments.

Actually, my inquiry led me on a different and more simple course. Ethan, as I mentioned, had sugar diabetes, which in his later years appeared to worsen. He became more and more fretful and sophomoric. I knew that he wasn't always in the best physical and mental condition because of the sugar, particularly when he abused its dietary regimen. I also realized that because he was not the best keeper of himself and had no continuous care and supervision, that that was often.

But surely Mt. Holly, part of whose general charge is to put its arms around the mentally, morally and physically disabled, wouldn't discriminate against its own, including its own pastor, would it? It was talked about around town that some church members thought that Ethan was at times child-ish and immature, but having no history of exaggerated mood swings and erratic behaviors that put into peril his ability to function, his sugar diabetes could not have been the ultimate problem, I reasoned.

Put differently, if it was at all true, Ethan's poor health should never have been confused with what was advertised as pastoral and personal failure, most assuredly, not something for which church floggings were compensation. To have dragged him through scrap piles of public scandal, charging him with ineptness wasn't fair. It would have been the more right thing for the church to have simply said: "Reverend Lam, we want to go in a different theological and leadership direction, and think you should. How can we make the transition a good one for us and for you?" Even if a polite way of saying, we don't want you anymore, this approach would have been more right, more morally consistent with Christian theology.

The whole Mt. Holly ordeal was like a surreal sequel of unabated horrors for Ethan. Through no shortage of righteousness and moral character, he hadn't made the grade at Coply or Shilah, and was now being tarred and feathered at Mt. Holly, his birthing church. It made me think back to that unwelcome business I experienced when trying to get back to St. James to say thanks. Namely, I wasn't the only one for whom returning to his home church wasn't exactly a "get out the fatted calf" welcome. It wasn't that for Ethan, only his return home was more than a sought after ten minute thanks' denial. It was a career, a dream, and a life that wasn't welcomed.

7

Covenants, Not Forever, After All

Alongside the downward spiraling of Ethan's pastorate at Mt. Holly, the mortar that once cohered the Lam family, or was thought to have, was breaking up. Ethan's family and church had coexisted in a precarious, though functionally supportive, relationship with each other. What fulfillment he couldn't realize in one, he sought in the other, shuttling back and forth in an ongoing effort to make sense out of his world. Neither could now be trusted for comfort when the other failed. As the church affair had been so unjustifiably repressive, his immediate family had some answers to give. His wife didn't just betray him at Mt. Holly, she humiliated and vilified him at home.

With accusations of inadequacy continuing to headline his life, I was bent on getting at the bottom of it all, of untangling the contiguous webs of abuse and deterioration therein. I asked Ethan to walk me through the rooms of his house, literally and figuratively. He consented, and he actually seemed relieved that I wanted to take the inquiry to this level. He slowly escorted me through each room, letting me peek into the deeper sanctuaries of his mind and soul. He told me things seen only on soap operas and read in fiction, giving me the frightening feeling that I was a character witness in another man's nightmare.

His voice shuttering, he pointed out an assortment of moral contaminants in and around the house, otherwise known as covenant violations. Soiled linen in closets and hampers, surprise guests with whom the ease of laughter could be heard through the hollow walls, suspicious scenes his zoom lens captured in his driveway and audio excerpts of *run away conversations, running wild,* were among them. It was a shockingly revealing tour, one where *I didn't take off my shoes, for there was no burning bush and holy ground on which I stood, and from where God spoke.* Ethan had been exiled into a bedroom next to his wife's, on which door she installed locks and refused to give him keys. This was more than a temporary measure of spousal discontent or transitory period of intimacy deprivation. It was permanent. For the last twenty years of his life, he lived in involuntarily celibacy, having no sense what it was like to feel the warmth of a woman standing or lying next to him—his wife, of course. Like a man who may on occasion openly glorify God for the sacredness of marital bliss, including the ecstasy of sexual intercourse, Ethan could render no such praise. Quarantined much like a Brahman class "untouchable," he could only weep, circumscribed to the lower bunks of sexual, moral and existential negation.

His nights, all of which began at the proverbial midnight hour, whatever time he went to bed, were spent in this emotionally empty room next door, a room whose companions were mere fantasy images of yesterday, and whose décor was signs posted over its walls, "morning, come quickly." As those who suffer with throbbing migraine headaches are sometimes pushed to the threshold of primal screaming, Ethan similarly shouted as loud as he could from the corners of his dungeons of despair, qualified by torturous loneliness and isolation. He sought to camouflage these pains by pulling the bed covers over his head no matter how hot the room during summers, pushing them off no matter how cold during winters.

He drifted near the portals of destruction. Unable to share his life with the woman in the next room, his whole body went into volcanic tremors every time he heard the clanging, clicking lock noises on its door. For these were indications that an un-welcomed husband couldn't come in, that imprisonment was not only punishment for the guilty but for the righteous, those having no idea what they may have done wrong.

Ethan's night lock-ups were interrupted with furloughs out into the free world by day, but he was still a prisoner, unable to unshackle himself from misery. Heavy steel balls chained to inmates when out on work detail were symbolically linked to Ethan's, slowly dragging him to closure. He was a victim of chained melody, unable to touch or be touched or to hold or be held. He could only love and not be loved in return. His lashings at Mt. Holly paled by comparison to those he got at home, as Mrs. Lam continued belittling him as an inadequate husband and of being less than a man.

From the same counselors and friends he had sought help regarding his troubles at Mt. Holly, he called on again. He pleaded with his wife in their presence to openly reveal her feelings on where he had done wrong—but to no avail. She was either mute, or just avoided or sidestepped things, those pursuant to possible resolution. Whenever she did choose to verbalize a reply, she said: "You know what you have done! He knows what this is all about. He knows . . . !" she would say. In one of the sessions she even said to Ethan, "I hate you." These words hurt him from every inch of his height to pound of his weight. There is nothing worse for a man or woman, who loves the other, to hear than words of covenant disaffirmation, most of all, "I hate you"—nothing. Not only was the thrill now gone, the (her) love was, replaced by its antipodal opposite, hate.

As Mrs. Lam had freed herself from Ethan physically in the house and emotionally in the relationship, she withdrew from his religious world. She stopped attending Mt. Holly, only showing up when it was time to pick up Ethan's paycheck, and to occasionally have a chat with the old deacon. She united with a denominationally independent church on Pittsfield's West Side, a stone's throw from Mt. Holly. Black folks in the city were up in arms, as embarrassed for Ethan as he was for himself, another stress-inducing load of distress to go with that which was already weighting him to the ground. I suppose one never gets used to carrying unwanted baggage, but Ethan had fewer and fewer choices regarding his. The African American religious saying, " . . . the Lord will not put more on us than we can bear . . . " had me wondering.

The "West Side story," as I identify it, would contribute to Ethan's tarnished story of agony in three additional ways. The first had to do with marriage counseling that Ethan consented to have with West Side's pastor, for all intents and purposes, his wife's pastor. With reconciliation efforts having run amuck, he was prepared to do anything and go anywhere for help, even a few blocks away to his wife's church. He remained deeply in love with her, as he had with his church, despite both their undeniable overtures of rejection. He felt that going to West Side, however, might give his wife a greater measure of comfort, that she might be more response-specific.

Ethan attended only two sessions, but he refused to go to others because of a conspicuously obvious counseling bias that hammered him for spousal negligence and inefficacy, notions taken right off the Mt. Holly press. He indicated that these were not meetings for marriage healing; they were friendly offensive forums for Mrs. Lam and "slap on the hand" reprimands by West Side's pastor for him being a poor husband and "so-so" pastor.

To be willing to go to a minister whom your wife prefers over you, to whom you are then asked to open up your soul to try to salvage your marriage, is something that only those having unusual guts could pull off, in the first place. It is not a gender matter by any stretch of the imagination, but I have often wondered what the outcome would be if women were placed in similar situations. If they were asked by their husbands to go to another woman for marriage counseling, to a woman in whom their husbands had shown personal and/or ecclesiastical preference. Hmm!

The second was that Mrs. Lam was sharing part of Ethan's income in West Side's offering baskets without his knowledge or consent. As such, she was not only profaning the ritual of covenant giving; Ethan was helping to pay for it, the profanation, that is. No one would contend that Christian stewardship isn't an act of personal volition, only that it be consciously done to reflect relational accountability. To have selected a church thought to have more palatable ministry than the one your husband pastor's, flaunting it around Pittsfield as the way ministry is to be done, may not qualify as the greatest insult to a marriage. But to use even part of a spouse's income to help defray its cost comes close.

This situation has caused me to rethink an old tradition on cross-church affiliation in the African American church, where unless it was certifiably clear that candidates coming to join were un-churched, black pastors would not allow them to unite with their congregations. These persons would need to be accompanied by a "letter of good standing" from their former church. It was a practice that might have been a little extreme, particularly because of its potential in stifling individual freedom. But the intent made sense. It served as a constraint on church-hoppers carrying membership aspirations from one church to another when feeling the urge.

The third had to do with de-commissioning Ethan from Christian fellowship. Talks had been in the works to have an annual Easter celebration between his church, Mt. Holly, The West Side Church, and a prominent East Side congregation. East Side's pastor and Ethan were enthusiastically in favor of the proposal, while the pastor of West Side vetoed it. His explanation was that he couldn't have fellowship with a minister who was not the head of his house . . . Huh? A decline to have an *Easter service* with a minister, about whom there was no material evidence of moral or theological impropriety, which, even if there is, no branch of reconciliation to extend to the fallen? *What up wit dat?* The tri-church Easter fellowship was off, plunging the knife of humiliation further into Ethan's already over punctured and profusely bleeding wounds. He took this hard, what was another prejudicial and baseless act of shame. The doors of his world were becoming increasingly heavy, closing in on him from every side—from his home and his church, and now the possibility that he was being locked out of Christian fellowship. Granted, this latest act of ecclesiastic punishment was from a pastor who had improperly and wrongly judged him, but would these closed doors be a prelude for what was to come, was the question? Would others find ways to ostracize him from praising God with them, and when exactly would all this senseless church and family authored brutality end?

His church and family had truly been out of control infernos, spewing cursing, mocking, and ill-defined recriminations at him at will: "You know what you have done." "You are not the man of your house . . ." etc. Now the flames were being blown by other winds, a living hell for Ethan, one in which he was a hopelessly distraught immigrant in and out of his own consciousness.

While this maddening travail in my brother's life revalidated my notion that he was a saint, it also gave me the sobering realization that the plots of evil hastening his rendezvous with death were thickening.

Meanwhile, I was still in the hunt for more revealing insights concerning the source of Ethan's trials, and I would explore every conceivable angle in the process. On the pivotal question of what he had or had not done, and what he did or did not know, as regards the nefarious charges he faced, I had become wearily dissatisfied. I most certainly wasn't happy with what I had heard from his accusers, but also, for the first time, not what I heard from him. It wasn't that I had lost confidence or trust in him; I just felt that there was more that he wasn't telling me, or that maybe even he wasn't fully aware of. Since his wife and those at the church were adamant in their insistence that he knew precisely what he had done, and had convinced others to accept their assessments, I now wanted to know what they knew.

I deduced that there is no doubt that Ethan wanted answers to the source of his nagging moral dilemma, but *not* necessarily to the questions he raised to get them. Things for which he really wanted answers, he didn't know how to ask. These were things having to do with sex, including his own sexuality. More than just being embarrassingly awkward, to ask them would have called into question his pristine understandings on the subject, something he wouldn't particularly want known. Don't forget: Ethan had had nothing comparable to a Worcester Avenue boot camp before marriage.

Ethan was church wise, but not street savvy. Hanging out on the corner where the *bloods* talked as openly about sex as they did about each other's mama was a world that Ethan never entered. This is not to imply that street seminars on sex are prerequisites for its informed and sufficient orientation, certainly not for covenant relationships. No convincing case can be made for brothers and sisters whose sex

70

education came from the streets as being better off than those who got theirs from other places. The point is: What might have been a frame of reference to accept or reject informal stoop training on the question, since there was no other kind available, was not something that Ethan could even draw on.

Ethan was sexually uninformed and may have been ridiculously naïve. He was almost Victorian, in which ideal typical definition it is anathema to discuss sex, sadly not even with one's husband or wife. This, along with him being hampered by diabetes-induced frigidity, shed important light on how his marriage's drop into the quagmire of no return may have occurred, at least in part. The question, "What have I done?" should have more likely been, "What *can* I sexually do, and that, within the limits of morally acceptable standards?" "Are there boundaries for married Christian sex? If so, what are they?" "If not, what aren't they?" "Are these even questions that I can ask?"

Simply, Ethan was seeking directives regarding sex in marriage. He wasn't asking the question what he had done wrong, but what could he do that was right. And since no two people can be given a patented prescription on sexual behavior that is uniformly functional, he was seeking a biblical O.K. approval or disapproval for what, in principle, might be sexually embraced by him, and by him and his wife.

He wanted to know what his colleagues were doing right—literally, what they were doing right in their bedrooms. To have received guidance from men whom he held in high esteem, to know what they did and how, and what he could do and how, was what he was after. How important it would have been for him to get a grip on bedroom etiquette, which, let's say for sake of discussion, and on the other side of the argument, he had betrayed his wife *and* himself in not diligently exploring.

His wife turned up the heat, or turned it down on him, depending on how you look at it. She wanted him to be more creative in the bedroom, and he had promised her he would, at least that he would try. But he couldn't pull it off. He couldn't do it early in the marriage because he didn't know how, and he was sex shy and reticent. He couldn't do it later because—well, he just couldn't. The sugar had done vicious and irreversible damage to his once more virile functions. Like being in the wrong place at the wrong time, it was a case of bad sugar, bad sex—I guess.

Being so uninformed about sex and marriage, and doing so little to stay in touch with their natural metamorphoses, Ethan was stumbling in the dark. There were essentially two aspects to his dilemma: one was the nature and range of sexual possibilities. Like an undetected or misdiagnosed illness, for which no medication, or the wrong one is prescribed, the counselors to whom he went for "please help" remedies were useless. Either his cry was not signaled to them, or it was a subject that they, too, were either uneasy or unqualified to broach. Given the theological persuasion in their backgrounds, and the cultural macho mystique regarding sex among African American males, it is not terribly shocking that they couldn't guide him. Of course, there is always the possibility that they had their own bedroom problems.

The second had to do with the implications of instrument-aided sexual intercourse, voluntarily introduced into the mix by Ethan because of the diabetes. He underwent "too little, too late" corrective surgery in order to come to terms with this disease, another wasted attempt to do whatever offered hope of bailing his marriage out of hoc.

Even though we were closer than blood, Ethan couldn't even raise this question with me, at least not its particularities. I have wished a thousand times he had. One part of me says that had he been more forthright, he could have spared himself years of disappointment and pain, because in all fairness, he, too, had the opportunity to blurt it out in counseling. But, I don't know. Another part of me says something different, that if the lack of knowledge and counsel on sexuality helped to destroy his marriage, given its convoluted and out of control covenants, I am not sure that having the most astute and informed counsel could have saved it. I say this, because covenants preserve marriages; counseling, techniques and perspectives on sex are their supplemental and enhancing tools, like props. If couples rely on them, there will inevitably be difficulties. If they believe the lines in their covenants, there can be *peace in the valley,* despite threatening disturbances on the mountain.

In any case, as I contended that health-related problems should not have constituted the basis for Ethan's unfair treatment at Mt. Holly, I feel even stronger regarding their role in taking the marriage down. This sugar disorder, effecting his sex activity and bedroom manners, along with his naiveté and timidity about them, didn't warrant the vituperative rejection by *madam.* Really, they didn't. Couples can learn to live with an unannounced and sudden paralysis, an unexpected debilitating disease, an un-welcomed physical incapacitation, and prolonged medically and socially based impotency. What may have once been a vibrant sex life for them could be precipitously reduced to a virtually no sex life at all. But this doesn't have to terminate marriages, or lead to their abridgement. Quite the contrary, when seen through covenant lens, transformation of what once was, to what is and can be, is imminently real, rich and fulfilling.

Ethan's mis- and un-education on sex was his albatross. The concept of marriage, something he once knew and honored more than life itself, had now become null and void. He was like a sheep being taken to slaughter, slowly and definitively pulled to the gate opening. And while he didn't quite go passively, as Jesus didn't on his way to Calvary, in the words of the old African American (dialectic) Easter hymn, " . . . Ethan never said a mumblin' word . . . ".

8

The New York Confessions
and Ethan's Death

Ethan accepted an invitation to visit me in New York, in the late '80s. While there, he emptied out more pain and clutter than even he knew had amassed over the years. I had never seen him so down. He seemed to have accepted the fact that these aggravating demons, unless countered with divine, direct, and immediate intervention, would drag him into eternity before time.

The pejorative chronicles of his accusers' claims wouldn't go away, the ones shoved in his face from God's house and from his. Since he had failed in getting candidates to share culpability in his trails of sorrows, he now pointed the finger of indictment inward. He wasn't asking them where he went wrong, but he was asking himself that. I tried walking him back through his life and the Bible that he had so scrupulously kept in moral and theological balance over the years. I wanted to assure him that he hadn't failed, that he, more than anyone I knew, was an integrated composite of courage and righteousness. I wasn't sure he heard me.

We talked for the whole night, what would actually be his valedictorian address, the closing summation of his journey. It was probably the longest night of his life, one in which he revealed an even more startling account of abuse and rejection, as if I didn't know enough already. Tearfully, he unbound ream after gory ream. He told me that it wasn't just on those occasions with counselors that his wife said she hated him; but when she did talk with him, and that was infrequent, she repeatedly told him the same thing in the privacy of their home. She told him that she would never love him, (again?) that it was forever over.

But Ethan still loved her. He wanted her more than he wanted his own life, and he never tired of doing the right spousal thing as its evidence. His epic descriptions of how much he yearned for reconciliation was the topic of his every waking moment, defining moments in which incredible pain and agony were transcended only by love at its highest possible level. He politely extended daily morning and nightly greetings to his wife, though usually without a response. He continued to courteously ask her about her well-being, and regularly made overtures for marriage renewal—dramatic, token, trial, any kind. He would have even accepted reconciliation with a tutor if necessary. It was not to be. It was not to be.

The prominent roles in Ethan's story were now being played by moral and covenantal will, not emotional, physical, or even spiritual ones. It was like those inspirational chapters in history that show heroic behavior in the face of natural and moral impossibilities. Ethan managed to inhale his wife's hate for him and exhale his love for her in the same breath, conflicting emotions that had become accustomed to growing diametrically in his life, like bad weeds wrapped around good grass.

The abject sadness with which he told me his episodes of horror was overwhelming. We talked for seven non-stop hours the second night, though I was not as strong a listener as he was a talker. I wanted to go to bed, perhaps to pull those old blankets he had used back in Pittsfield, covering him from pain and shame, over my own head. But I refused to give into a pilgrimage of denial. I realized that the volcanic mass of debilitating anxiety, this unbridled distress couldn't wait, that if the ferocity of unleashed hell hounds were permitted to senselessly bite at him another minute, that there would be no hope, not even "joy cometh in the morning" palliatives, of saving him. I stayed with the course through the night, and tried to just *rock his soul in the bosom of Abraham.*

Ethan told me that he could count the words on one hand that he and his wife exchanged in the course of weeks, months, then years. The physical segregation of living in separate rooms in the house was a love ballad comparable only to the deadening walls of un-communication and indignant silence they shared betweem them. Their worlds had irreversibly drifted far apart. The religion that once had them praying at the same formal altars was now being separately practiced, as though their God's name and character had changed, unrecognizable as the one to whom they once said "I do" together. Their circles of friends and activities were entirely different now, and they would never cross fraternizing and fellowship paths again.

As we talked into the third day, he told me about a parade of uninvited people and events to and around his house, including unexplained and frequent visits from the Chicago official who married them. What he told me he witnessed him doing, as he peeked through the kitchen window in the driveway one evening, was riveting. The harshest description he could think of was to refer to the minister as "that Negro . . . ", one that may have been more than adequate; given the ominous place this term now has for most African Americans.

Ethan also hadn't been clear with me on another matter. Casually mentioning an alleged rumor regarding another pastor's wife's gender indiscriminate unfaithfulness in town, I now suspect that he was speaking circumlocution. More embarrassed than with anything he ever told me, there is compelling suggestion that he was really talking about his own worst domestic fantasy. The famous children's riddle,

" . . . somebody's been sittin' in my chair, eatin' at my table and sleepin' in my bed" was his own night song, one whose moan and groan rhythm he had learned on the second floor of the old house back at Dodge Street.

The most shocking disclosure of all was Ethan's revelation that he had bugged his own telephone. He made himself privy to more than a year's worth of unedited telephone conversations, graphically depicting his failures and impotency. He listened to those he loved and in whom he placed trust have field days on him, viciously messing with his sanity and manhood. It was one thing to have been an innocent bystander to humiliating tirades with him as subject; it was another to directly monitor them on tape, which to add injury to insult once more, he was paying the monthly phone bills, financially subsidizing his own brutal emasculation, if you will.

These recordings were like exploding shrapnel in his soul, breaking into a thousand pieces with every demeaning word and sound of demonic laughter, disguised in human utterance. Occasionally pulling his car over to some of Pittsfield's dark back roads, shielding himself from public recognition, he listened to these tapes, over and over again he listened. He was like a junkie hiding in a dim lit tenement stairwell administering a fix, only for Ethan someone else was forcing the toxin into his arteries, the arteries of his soul. Rivers of devastation filled his already overrun water banks—so twisting his mind, so shocking his innocence, so decimating his self concept, that it's a wonder he could have lived another day. But he did. He lived what must have seemed like an eternity *each* day, as snippets of decomposed insignificance were stapled to his psyche until it ran out of space for more.

His self-esteem plummeted to its lowest levels. I made him terminate these recordings. I knew that they could finally take him out, that he might one day be found dead in his car from an overdose of despair. But how could he erase their messages from his mind? How could he forget, and how could he forgive? I don't know. I don't know, that is, if he forgot. I only know that he forgave, and he was inevitably prepared to do so again and again, if only provided an opportunity.

Deterioration was setting in all over the place. He no longer had an income from rent payments on the property on the East Side. His wife had urged him to sell it years earlier. The Laundromat folded and he had left the barbering business. The only income he had was his from Mt. Holly, to me the only real inadequacy in that relationship, which he augmented with a weekday job at the Pittsfield County Community Action Agency.

Some people advised him to pack his bags and leave, but that was out of the question. Not for the typical reasons that lawyers tell estranged spouses not to leave the house. He could not leave because the best part of his theology had no room for separation and divorce, only patience and forgiveness. Each of his disparate worlds showed increasing intolerance for the other, for not running him stone out of his mind. He was not schizophrenic on these contradictory paths of destiny, but if not frequently seen in an entourage of angels, he could very easily have been.

This critical New York visit, in which we talked into the closing chapter of the Ethan Lam story, would come to an end, though I was determined to stay in closer touch. I called him at least once a week, sometimes more. I found it increasingly difficult getting in touch with him, when he was not at home to directly answer the phone. He wasn't always given my messages. More and more, I didn't want to leave them.

I went to Pittsfield and picked him up to travel with me to Chicago for some business in the fall of 1994. Once again, we talked. For nearly two days straight, we talked. When returning him to Pittsfield, I urged him to get another phone in the house, that his friends needed to be assured of getting in contact with him, and so did I. He did. I told him to get someone to regularly wash and iron his clothes and to prepare him meals consistent with his dietary regimen, and that I would pay. Those glitteringly clean and liquid starched-ironed white shirts he used to wear were now hung dried, dingy and collar ringed. One of the most difficult things I ever told him was how he had let himself go, how he had permitted his personal upkeep to deteriorate. I ached deeply about this, but he was my brother. I had to tell him. He seemed embarrassed, but he understood.

I wanted him to come and spend a few weeks in New York again, just so we could take care of him for a while, wait on him hand and foot. He never did.

In 1995, he had a sugar-related blackout spell, and he was forbidden to drive the agency van. An emergency occurred and, with no one else available, he drove it anyway. As a result, his superior pressured him to resign, a legal case he seemed close to winning before he died. It would be lost after he did. He was now essentially jobless. Once a proud and financially independent man, he wasn't many steps away from poverty. He talked of selling his van because he couldn't make its payments. I was saddened.

Ethan was more shut off from friends and colleagues than ever. For the first time, he seemed resigned to the fact that his wife would never be part of their covenant equation again, scars from which realization had so disfigured him, he didn't look or sound like the same person.

In late November of 1996, we went to breakfast at a local East Pittsfield restaurant, for what would be another of our many such times of reflection. We must have had hundreds of them over the years, but this would be our last. His own problems aside, still so typical of him, he was concerned about those of a friend, a friend who had been reported to be involved in some unsavory activity on the other side of town, an affair. Ethan asked me if he should pull the brother's coattail. I told him not to, that he was old enough, and had been around the corner enough times, to know what he was doing. Ethan was O.K. with that and never mentioned it.

He told me at this breakfast meeting that he wanted to go back to Africa and work under me. This was an interesting disclosure. Leave Pittsfield? I didn't ask what this meant, though knew that no divorce consideration was in the offing. I was just elated at the prospect that we might do some work together again. I corrected his wording, work *under* me, however. I told Him that he could most definitely come to the continent to work *with* me, just like the old days, campaigning on the urban trail together—in this case, in the rural bush together.

In mid-December of 1996, he made one last-ditch effort to get himself and Mt. Holly in an ecclesiastically workable arrangement. This one would include the church congregation voting on the matter. One way or the other, he wanted referendum on his leadership, sort of like what happens in Israel politics that allow for elections when the peoples' confidence in the government has eroded. Mt. Holly's members who hadn't been to church in years would come and cast their ballots. It was voting time. "All those in favor of keeping Reverend Lam on as our pastor, raise your hands!" Members slipped their hands into the air, each curiously looking around the room to get a glimpse of the outcome. The count was a majority not in favor of retaining Ethan. It was over.

As his personal marriage was morally and unofficially over, his pastorate was, technically and officially. His time was at hand. *Judas had kissed him on the cheek, singling him out as an unworthy prince to the lynch mob that had come to apprehend him, to lead him to the gallows.*

It was an awful defeat from which Ethan would not recover—that is, from that fateful New Year's Eve when the death angel came a knockin' at his back door, too ashamed to come to the front because there was not enough evidence for him to call Ethan to glory. Ethan wouldn't get off the mat from the sound of the whip against his emaciated spirit, a sound that could be heard from one side of Pittsfield to the other, from one side of the Atlantic to the other. It's been more than four years now. I can still hear it wherever in the world I am.

We spoke on the phone on December 26th, two weeks later. He was in pieces, though like a defeated man who doesn't realize he is, he tried to rally. He said to me, "Chester, I am going to give them one more chance . . . " I was confounded. He hadn't gotten it; he had been handed his final walking papers, his head on a platter, and he just hadn't gotten it. He was dying softly, but not sweetly. He would have never consciously done physical harm to himself, but he appeared unbearably close to committing moral suicide, if for no other reason than by default. I pleaded with him to leave it, to just leave it. I reminded him that he could come to Africa with me as he had indicated he wanted to do. He was silent.

Ethan had never said this before, but he acknowledged that he might have been out of the will of God in either staying at Mt. Holly too long or in having gone there in the first place. He was so fragile and hurt, I dared not comment, particularly in the strict sense in which he expressed this possibility. I also ultimately knew that I had no basis to respond, having only thought of him and Mt. Holly as incompatible in the beginning of that relationship, and that going to a church in which one was nurtured as a child, to lead as an adult, is risky business.

The betrayals and abuses had finally caught up with my brother—a wife, a church, some friends, and a job that no longer needed or wanted him. In the words of Dionne Warwick's classic, "Who Can I Turn To, When Nobody Needs Me?" was once again Ethan's cry. It was a loin cry, emitting sounds of agony that only those in communion with God can hear. I do not claim to be one of these special hearers, but I think that in this moment I came close.

I left for Africa on December 28, and I checked into the Apollo Hotel in Gambia. Two days later, after having gone to my room and taken off my clothes for bed, there was a knock on my hotel room door. It was an employee who had come to let me know that there was an international call for me. I was nervous, sensing something was wrong, because there would be no reason for a call coming into me at that hour. I quickly dressed and ran downstairs to answer. I could feel my heart beating loudly against my chest wall, like a resonating dong from Sunday morning church bells. Who and what was it?

It was our teenage friend, Lawrence—Ethan's and mine. My mind raced faster than my awareness could keep pace. It sped through all the possibilities as to why he would want to speak with me—in Africa. Then, in a fragment of second, I eliminated everything and everybody except one, Ethan! Lawrence greeted me and said in a quiet, subdued voice: "It's Ethan, Chester. He had a massive stroke. He is hospitalized, and it doesn't look good for him."

Ethan! I momentarily lost my balance and became instantly disheveled. Ethan! My brother! "What happened?" I asked. As coherently as he could, Lawrence struggled with a reply. He told me what he had heard, that while eating breakfast, he slumped over into a paralyzing stroke. Cognizant of how inseparably close we were, and how I would likely be affected at such news, Lawrence tried to be comfortingly near to me, having to simultaneously grapple with his own pain. He was as "stand up" in courage at that time as one can be. I have thanked him several times for how he so graciously handled all this.

It seemed to take forever for the news to make its way into my consciousness, slowly pausing at various stops on that thirty-five-year road of unbroken, brother to brother, relationship. This was the road on which we had traveled through days of joyous laughter and painful disappointments, the bumpy terrain over which he had so graciously brokered my own personal midnights, and where his presence had been larger than life itself. Now, at this confusing juncture, our road of engagement had become a mixture of scattered debris, an unlikely prospect that my (our) future may not include him.

Twenty-four hours later, the second call came. The plug had been pulled. Ethan was dead.

I grabbed the rail near the phone housing when getting the news, barely able to see past the sheets of tears rapidly rolling down my face. I slowly climbed the steps and stumbled back into my room. I fell limp to my knees and began to pray. I am not sure what I said; I just cried and prayed. I guess this was one of those times in the Christian experience where the Holy Spirit just takes complete charge, receiving and translating what you think you want to say to God, and what you think you want God to hear. But you aren't sure. You are so utterly helpless. All you know is that you are "... *leaning on {His} everlasting arms* ...".

Having passed that phone stand at the hotel probably a hundred times since, I still can't comfortably talk on it, as though it was yesterday when getting the news about Ethan.

When calls come in for me these days, I reach for it with fear and trembling. I sometimes think that I hear it ringing in my room on an upper floor, but it isn't ringing at all. I guess "... *it is just my imagination, running away with me.*"

The most human part of me ached beyond description. What would I do? How would I handle all this turmoil, especially on a distant continent and unable to be empathetically near understanding fellow mourners? But I knew that I had to shake my sorrows. While my best friend, the young towering prince of righteousness, was dead, I had come to Africa to fulfill *my* calling, to deliver supplies and messages of hope for the New Year to our friends, to our brothers and sisters. There were four villages on the North Bank in the Gambia waiting for me, and God had sent me to serve them. Ethan, one of His children, my brother, wouldn't have it any other way.

On New Year's morning, I managed to pull myself together. I showered, though uncertain when or how I dressed myself, and boarded the ferry to cross the Gambia River. Still dazed, I went to our Barra complex and announced to our staff what had happened. I indicated that we would go to the villages as planned, but that I would need to leave immediately for Senegal after that and try to get a flight back to the States.

We put finishing touches on the trip, readying ourselves to take clothing and medical supplies to our friends. We were warmly greeted upon our arrival. I shared the *good news* of the gospel. In each of these waiting outdoor assemblies where our friends heard of my brother's death, the greeting was an orchestrated moan, as only Africans can do when wanting to show deep emotions. They have a special cry for those who have experienced death. Their sympathetic facial expressions, placing their hands over their mouths when uttering, *Ohh!* brought me relief. There is no place on the planet I would rather be than in Africa, or among African peoples, when needing a human embrace in times like these.

Meanwhile, I was in contact with Lawrence regarding Ethan's funeral. When learning that the plans did not include me as eulogist, nor ceremonially doing anything else, and that it would not be held up an extra day for my arrival, I sought a redress, a way that I could express my testimony of my best friend. Lawrence said he would do his best to pull together whatever I wanted.

I suggested that we have a memorial the day after the funeral, that he should see if Larry C. Cummings would allow us to use his church, the North Side Baptist Church. Reverend Cummings agreed. Lawrence put the announcement of my coming and the planned memorial on local television and in the newspapers. As he was taking care of these matters, I knew that I needed to concentrate on getting back. I figured that if I couldn't get out on Air Afrique because of my special ticket, I would just have to charge an additional one on another airlines and go up through Europe. I would think about how to pay for it later.

I left the Gambia for Senegal, usually a rough six-hour ride over some of the worst roads in Africa. This time I was numb to its rocky ride and jarring road craters. The mini-car driver, like most of them on this Gambia/Senegal run, seemed to be out of control most of the way, speeding and recklessly changing lanes when doing so most dangerously affects the safety of passengers. We actually ran head on into a dirt embankment on this trip. I didn't seem to mind.

When we arrived in Dakar, I got a taxi and went directly to Yoff Airport. I knew that I was there on the wrong day to get an Air Afrique flight to New York, but I went anyhow. I entered the terminal and was immediately met by an airport solicitor who knew that I frequently travel to and from the States. He told me that the plane for New York was leaving in an hour. I was surprised. Air Afrique was not supposed to leave until the following day. I hurried to the counter, anxiously looking for a friend who works for the airlines. *"Est ce que madam Daba est la?"* I asked. *"Oui, elle est la,"* the attendant replied. Daba was there. I felt that if there were any chance at all, she would make it happen for me. I ran to her office, told her that my brother had died, and that I needed to get back to New York right away. I didn't inquire why the plane was headed for JFK Airport on this unscheduled day. I didn't care. I just wanted to be on this one.

She expressed her sympathies and went directly to the computer, searching for me a seat. There was one. My heart thumped with gratitude. She took care of the whole thing without my incurring a penalty. I began to utter a series of "thank you, Lord's." In less than an hour, I was en route to New York.

I have made this trans-Atlantic flight probably eighty times, and confess I am generally uneasy when flying over the Atlantic, especially through unremitting turbulence. This time was different. I didn't have stomach jitters and felt no nervous twitches when bobbing up and down in deep air pockets. I was at peace. I prayed, stared out the window, occasionally jotted down a few notes, and just talked to myself. I think I talked to Ethan, too. I know I talked to God.

9

Memorials: Fitting and Unfitting

When I arrived at JFK Airport, I went immediately to New York to collect some things for the memorial and left for Pittsfield. I anxiously wanted to hear how things had gone the day before, the day of the funeral. It was difficult to even imagine Ethan lying prostrate in a coffin. Not seeing or hearing him on his feet in a pulpit preaching, in a court-house testifying or in a rehabilitation center, counseling, was something I had never thought about, but I wanted to know how he looked, how he was dressed, whether he looked like himself, what songs were sang, and who said what. I was told that the church was overrun with well-wishers, and that fellow ministers and friends had come from far and near to pay respects to our fallen brother.

I was also provided a not-so-glowing report, one that included a bit of sinister sneering and giggling, and a kiss being placed on his forehead. I thought to myself: if only it had been put there when the blood ran warm in Ethan's veins, *"when the walls of his room were not the walls of his grave, and his bed was not his coolin' board . . . "* his life would have been so different. His death just may not have been at all—just one kiss on his face, anywhere, anytime . . . *if only.*

The service at North Side was well attended, probably 125 people. Most of those in attendance knew of Ethan's and my special relationship, specifically the eulogy covenant we had made as teens. They had gone to his funeral a little more than twenty-four hours earlier, but they had come again a day later to help heal my wounded spirit, and to take advantage of another opportunity to continue healing their own. Like "honey in the rock," as Mother Nelson used to say on the Pittsfield circuit, their being there filled a void in me that could not have been done by any other audience.

Ethan's two children came. His son's wife, whom most of us had never met, appeared especially sensitive to the meaning of the service. Without her realizing it, Pittsfielders had their eye on her and gave her high marks as they listened and watched her give grace, dignity, and respect to her father-in-law's memorial.

I reminded these friends of our joint history and of Ethan's utterly righteous life. I took them back to YCC days, to those moments we journeyed together to shape Pittsfield's only religious renaissance. When finished, I presented a U.S. flag to Ethan's mother to honor his military hitch and then called a few of his friends to join me in communion—no connection to a tradition thought to invoke the presence of the dead at such times. While I attach no theological significance to this fact, the bottle in which I poured the sacrament has not evaporated, four years later. From time to time, I look at it sitting on the top shelf in the kitchen cabinet. I smile holy when doing so.

Before closing the service, several shared recollections of Ethan, crying a lot, laughing some. These moments in ritualized catharsis went a long way in helping me to get a grip on things. I think they helped others, too.

The following morning I went to the cemetery, and I walked ever so reverently over to the freshly covered hole where his body lay. I asked to be alone, just to sort of talk to God and myself about Ethan, and to God and Ethan about me. When unable to hold it together, I belly groaned. I sobbed and I sobbed, just as I had done in Africa a few days earlier. While it was clearly over, I couldn't believe that it was. I just couldn't believe it.

I wanted something of Ethan's, a Bible, some of his books or his sermon notes, just for the memories. But these things would be given to a cross-racially admired evangelical white church, the church on Fox Hill. While there was nothing inherently wrong with this, its members wouldn't likely have a great appreciation for them; after all, they were not the lost sermons of Charles Spurgeon, a homiletic legacy closer to its theological tradition. We, his close friends, would have valued them more, having joyously labored with him. We were given nothing.

I returned to New York, but I stayed in touch with what was going on, and what I could possibly make go on.

It has been said that the best and worst in the human family can be seen when death occurs. Ethan's case was no exception. I had experienced the best at the memorial. When back home, I heard the worst, that the rest of Ethan's belongings were put on the street for the garbage collector, two days after his burial, and that before the last screech of the ratchet lowering his body into the ground, the race for his vacated pulpit was on. With bio-sketches in one hand, a Bible and song sheet in the other, some of the city's unemployed ministers lined up on Mt. Holly's doorsteps hoping to get the call. Many of them had been fellow ministers, had enjoyed the benefits of Ethan's helping presence in their own times of need and had just attended his funeral, ceremonially bemoaning his death. They were now groping, grabbing and groveling for the pulpit he had faithfully served in, and from which he was so routinely dismissed a few weeks earlier.

Ethan's successor was to have initially been an interim appointment for three months. He has lasted for nearly four years, a young minister whose apprenticeship came under Ethan, who had, in fact, been his assistant at one time. When Rev. Lowell flew in from Texas to the memorial ceremonies, he privately expressed outrage at what, according to him, " . . . *they* had done to his pastor." I was happy to learn that he shared our views regarding Ethan's mistreatment, and therefore surprised that he accepted the appointment so soon, without convening a solemn church assembly on the abuse of power in its "Amen corners," beforehand.

I suspect that Ethan would have had no misgivings in knowing that Reverend Lowell has succeeded him, though he might have suggested that there be a prior time of reflection—some mourning time, as the old folks used say, "some *moanin'* time."

Under his leadership, the psychology of Mt. Holly seems to have been to quickly move on with its affairs, erasing the Ethan Lam twelve-year tenure from its history. There is no photo of Ethan in the church narthex, no insert of his legacy on its walls, and little or no reference to him in its public conversations. Its choirs don't have him in mind as one of those whom God sent to take them over troubled waters when singing, "How I Got Over." How the church has managed to go on without having had institutionalized healing is curious, a course of inaction that either represents an unusual religious story of effortless atonement, or is a classic case of ecclesiastical denial.

Knowing a few of its courageous members, I wouldn't be shocked to hear one day that they will have exchanged their church clothes, powder puffs, and cologne splash for sack cloths and ashes, and decided to sit out on the church lawn in a holy uprising. For they will have come to the enlightened conclusion that some less than righteous activities went on in the church's back rooms and that biblically based justice for their former pastor got miscarried all the way to the doorsteps of unchecked evil and death. They will understand that only a sustained penitent petitioning the God of Abraham, Isaac, and Jacob, of Sarah, Ruth, and Esther can bring about church cleansing. In such a holy gathering, I would actually unite with them and would personally take off my cleric garb and put on temple garments of repentance.

One option I had at this juncture was to go away. The other was to try and concretize Ethan's memory in some sort of lasting testament. I asked a few of his friends if we could consider one more run, some work on a project to permanently memorialize Ethan. The response was good, as would be expected after losing one so cherished. With Ethan's mother's consent, we decided to have our meetings at her house. Lawrence and I thought that having them there would take us back to the days when so much of what we did under Ethan's leadership occurred. What better place than at this old stompin' ground to conduct planning sessions on a monument in his memory, to write his name onto the pages of western Pennsylvania's story.

Commuting to Pittsfield from New York for these gatherings meant a sixteen-hour roundtrip drive for me, something I didn't mind if those living fifteen to twenty minutes away would make a serious effort to attend, on time. At the first meeting, we proposed three things. One, Lawrence suggested that we have an annual memorial caravan to Barsdale Cemetery, New Year's Eve, the day Ethan died. Two, Maria Arlene, a longtime friend of Ethan's, indicated that we should develop The Ethan Lam, Jr. Memorial Foundation, for which she would do the legal work. I thought this was a great idea and wanted its proceeds to be used for international missions; she wanted them to also reflect local concerns. Three, I proposed that we start legal and community awareness procedures to have Nat Street, where he lived most of his life, renamed after him. This was to have included a back to school festival for the local neighborhood, a rally at North Side Church for the city as a whole and eventually a diligent pursuit of the appropriate political people to lobby for the idea with city hall.

It was basically a good meeting, with our sharpest differences centering on the question of whether to invite Ethan's wife to subsequent ones. We never resolved that issue, though heatedly argued it. It was a dissension cloud that hung around for the rest of the group's brief history.

At our second gathering, Ethan's daughter came. I was especially concerned that being there could place her in an awkward position, privy to sensitive information, and all, and that she may not be able to handle it. She indicated that she was mature and that this would be no problem, though she would later verbalize disapprove of our activities, specifically my directing them. She felt that her father would not particularly like us jawing and jarring over his memory, and that she was representing his best interest in telling us so. She didn't attend subsequent meetings. I understood.

I would make this trip from New York to Pittsfield every three weeks, only to experience increasing absenteeism and tardiness because of other priorities, baby showers, grocery shopping, hair-dressing appointments, etc. Regarding hairdo's, I knew that I had absolutely no possibility of ever gaining the edge. African American women's hair and nail appointments will inevitably win out over all their competing attractions, even if rich Texas oil tycoons are reported to be giving away free money in the area.

With increasing group distrust, discord and misplaced animosity, the group was in trouble. I hurried things along as fast as I could. But it was too late, as I think back on it, probably too late from the beginning. The organization began to wane, with its members showing signs of becoming more and more disinterested and un-engaged. Applications to suspend a banner we had made with Ethan's name emboldened on it for the festival were filed late; we couldn't get a permit. We didn't get a promised mailing list of Pittsfield's black clergy, those we wanted to invite to the evening rally at North Side and we couldn't get a write up in the city's leading newspaper. This particular snag highlighted the hideously sad state of affairs in which our efforts were.

The news reporter had earlier indicated that he thought we had a story, and that he would run it. We were quite pleased with this because it would have been a tremendous boost in exposing greater Pittsfield to what we were doing. At the last minute he changed his mind, a decision I later had reason to believe was influenced by a local councilman, one through whose office the filing for street re-naming proposals had to initially go. It seems that he felt excluded because we hadn't crossed all of our "t's" and dotted all of our "i's" with his monitoring and participatory approval. I have always been motivated by the most elementary of political strategy, to sufficiently educate and mobilize the community before going to its elected leaderships. We had successfully elicited all but two residents on Nat Street to sign on to having the street renamed after Ethan, and we were well on our way. We would have brought this brother in later. Oh, well.

How ironic! First, the life was choked out of Ethan in his religious and personal marriages. Then the death was squeezed out of him by a writer at the city's leading newspaper, by an elected councilman over the district in which he lived and by some Pittsfielders unable to do the Quincy Jones, "check their individual egos at the door" for the larger good. With the educational street festival off, with no publicity in the media, and with no advertisement for the North Side Church rally, the project was a virtual flop.

I came back to New York stressed out, though a few months later returned to Pittsfield in order to facilitate the cemetery memorial. It would be my last initiative.

As we had always done when needing a dependable hand in getting things done, I called on Lawrence. Once again, he was there for me. He got an announcement in the newspaper, but he was unable to get a church location for us to have prayer, reflection, and conversation before heading for the cemetery. We tried the one nearest to Ethan's mother's house, but its elder was out of town, with no one authorized to grant permission for its usage in his absence. At the next closest church, we were refused because, according to the pastor, there was a deacons' meeting to be held there at 11:30 A.M. We wanted to meet at noon. I failed to see the relationship between this deacon's meeting and a twenty person gathering to pray, even if in a church hall or closet. This is a very large church with long-standing roots in the community, in fact, is the church home of Ethan's parents. Its pastor is also a Baptist and a member of the same metropolitan association in which Ethan was. I didn't understand. What was it? What was going on? Why was this long morally dirtied road on which Ethan was forced to walk circuitously winding its way into our paths? In my mind, there should have been no hesitation about letting a few Christians gather to pray for the memory of a colleague, just for a minute or two—in my mind. It just seemed that there was no place for Ethan to lay his head, not in life, not in death.

In any case, I concluded, no problem! We can go to mother Lam's. After our pre-memorial sharing, and about to leave for Bardsdale, I was told that we would have to wait for Norton because he was the only one who knew exactly where the grave was. I was mortified at this revelation, as well as the discovery that there was no stone at the grave. I think my anger showed.

When Norton arrived, we left, nine cars driving slowly to Barsdale with our lights on, carefully nudging our cars along the city's icy streets. Upon our arrival, we were greeted by a woman standing at what we assumed was the gravesite with a stick in her hand. She had used it to mark off in the three to four inches of gathered snow a rectangular, casket-size set of lines. Curiously, no one now seems to know who this woman was or where she can be found. In my theological fantasying, I have thought that maybe she was an angelic descendant of the women who made their way to the tomb of their friend Jesus in the first century. When they arrived they heard the news, ". . . He is *not* here. . . . " This Pittsfield sister, two thousand years later, made her way to the grave of her friend, Ethan. Our news from her was, "He *is* here . . ." I have never seen an angel, let alone heard one smile or cry. I just remember that her grin seemed larger than the woman's in a full moon.

Patricia brought flowers and shared them with us to lay on the area that we supposed housed Ethan's remains. We each placed them around the stick markings over him, though I learned later that we were a grave or two off the mark. That wasn't nearly as awkward to us as it was embarrassing for a weekly visiting mourner praying and crying over the wrong grave for a year. Of course, God knew his heart. Ethan would have found it hysterical, but not long afterwards would have affirmed the righteousness of his dear friend's intent.

After our personal reflections, I expressed deep concerns to his friends, as they stood shivering in single digit temperatures, about Ethan's stone-less grave. I told them that we must never again come to memorialize him having to guess where his body is and resort to lines drawn on the ground. I wasn't sure who heard or took my resolve seriously. But, in the telling cliché used by black youth, I was, indeed, that: *serious.*

When concluding the graveside memorial, I went by my mother's house and connected a U-Haul trailer to my jeep. I stopped at a fueling station on Worcester Avenue to gas up before heading back to the East Coast. On the opposite side of the island from where I stood was the minister who had denied us use of his church that morning. I don't think he recognized me because I had put on my traveling clothes. Few can identify me in those threads. There he stood, pumping gas into his tank, clean as the board of health, shiny pointed toe shoes, and all. I glanced over in his direction and at his huge car. Funny how black ministers' automobiles always seem to be about a foot longer than they really are, especially those with Cadillacs and Lincolns. I felt a little sad, a little disappointed, and a little angry, though I don't think that this elder statesman is a bad person for denying us a place to pray. He just made a bad call.

Since it was clear that I could no longer give direction to the committee, I asked Patricia to take over. I suspect that she did her best, though I never heard one way or the other. I do know that there have been no subsequent meetings, no Ethan Lam, Jr. Foundation talks, no street renaming activities and "no shows" for subsequent graveside memorials.

Most importantly for me, there was still no gravestone to mark the occasion of Ethan's presence on the earth, nor his remains in it. I returned to New York.

10

Laying the Stone and Raising the Saint

Along with concrete stones laid around Ethan's death, there are three interconnecting spiritual and figurative ones draped around his life. The first is theological. This is the stone, the Bible says, ". . . that the builders rejected . . ." Jesus Christ, the center and circumference of Ethan's world. It would be the one on which Ethan proudly stood to pronounce to all that would hear him that radical life transformation was possible when encountered by this Jesus. The second represented an adversarial corps of family and church folks. These were stones of relational support on which he relied to underpin his moral and theological will, but those that ended up tossing him from one pillar of rejection to another. The third stone symbolizes Ethan, himself. Despite the faltering connections around him, he was like a rock of resilience, firmly standing for and on his beliefs and covenants, irrespective of the sustained actions of others to render him weak, impotent, and useless.

Then there was the concrete monument I laid over Ethan's remains, in which initial project phases, I discovered that one can shop and bargain for gravestones like doing so for used cars. I saved $400 in doing so. I also learned that cemetery stratification, similar to that of society, has designated areas for different size and makeup of stones, upright stones, flat ones, mausoleums and the like. In other words, as wealth and power determine how and where we live, they do so with where our remains are buried when we die. Ethan is buried where flat stones are, on the less expensive side of the graveyard.

With the help of a friend, Lon Janks in Scotch Plains, New Jersey, I arranged to have the stone made in central New Jersey. When completed, March of 1998, I drove to New Jersey to pick it up. It was heavier than a small truck, but Lon and I attached it to a dolly and after some pulling, pushing, and muscle strains that I was certain would require a liniment rubdown, we loaded it into my jeep. I gathered my tools, a small garden pick, a hoe, a shovel, a trowel, some large black garbage bags, a rope, a hand truck, a tape measure, and a small bag of cement. I took off, driving hurriedly through the night, remembering the words of the late Erlene Jones, ". . . we must always be *duty bound . . . Chester!*" I was driven to be duty bound.

As I proceeded west on the Pennsylvania Turnpike, I could see a highway patrolman's lights flashing in my rearview mirror. I wasn't speeding, and couldn't figure out what was wrong. I immediately thought about the stone lying face up in the back of the jeep. On one side of it was a man-sized African wood sculpture, and on the other side was my Bible. You can imagine the suspenseful imagery here. How could I prepare the approaching officer for this, shall we say, unusual cargo if he flashed his light around inside? Thankfully, after reviewing my documents, he told me to stay out of the left-hand lane unless passing another vehicle. Wshhhssh!

The question was, who was I going to convince to help me lift Ethan's name out of irreverent grave soil, *out of the muck and mire,* and "stone" his life with goodness and grace? Finding people who would agree that it was shameful that there was no stone for him was one thing. Getting them to help me lay one for him was another. After going through a list of possible collaborators, I came up empty. I did think of approaching one of his close Jewish friends, feeling that his involvement wouldn't be suspect, but I subsequently changed my mind.

I was in a quandary, because this stage was taking on a complexity that seemed extraneous to what I had in mind. I just wanted to get a stone in the ground as soon as possible. I chose to not seek help from anyone. I would do it alone, *moi-meme*.

I arrived in Pittsfield, nervous and uneasy. I knew that laying the stone was not a felony, but that it was not exactly cooking squash for dinner either. In planning how to pull it off, I thought I'd mark off the prescribed 12x24-inch square over the grave during the day and return late at night to finish the job. I would pull up to the iron fence nearest the lot containing Ethan's remains and quietly throw over my bag of tools. I then reasoned that I would tie the 200-pound stone onto a rope, climb the iron fence, hoist it over, dolly-pull it to the site, and flash my little light onto the ground while digging. Hmmm! How was I going to pull that amount of weight up a fence, and how was I going to hold the light while digging and laying it at the same time? And what if, perchance, someone saw me and thought I was a grave robber, or worse, a lunatic?

I was beginning to get spooked. Here I am, a black man, driving a black jeep, maybe, on a rainy night—wearing a black ski cap, dragging a stone and sack on the ground through a graveyard. There would just be no way that I could explain to authorities that my intentions were good.

I decided to just drive into Bardsdale Cemetery on the ensuing Sunday morning and do it. It was a nice day, about 45 to 50 degrees. This meant that the ground wouldn't be frozen and too hard for digging. I measured the distance between the stones in the area to get an accurate read on where his coffin was buried, and then I marked off my digging area. With no one around, I got on my knees and drove my trowel about six inches down in the earth. *I hoped that its sounds would not disturb Ethan, that he would know they were friendly ones.*

I quickly dug out the dirt and poured a bag of cement into the hole, so that when the rains came and moistened the soil the stone would adhere. Monument people had given me this tip. I went to the jeep, lowered the stone to the ground, and pulled it to the hole. I slowly dropped it in. It was a near perfect fit. Had I megaphone, I would have shouted, "The stone is in place! Friends of the righteous, the stone is in place!" But I was by myself and could only shout it in my soul, though I felt so accompanied, so un-alone; you know what I mean?

I suddenly spotted two women pushing baby carriages, strolling leisurely in my direction. Why they were walking instead of being in a vehicle, I didn't know. With my tools lying around, what would I do if they got close and curious? They would most certainly see the newly laid stone and might have become a little more inquisitive than I was prepared to give even the slightest response to. I started loudly singing, "Blessed Assurance," so they would think that I was in mourning, which I was of course, but I wanted them to know it. As they walked by with barely a glance in my direction, I breathed a sigh of relief. I then filled in around the edges of the stone, scooped up the remaining dirt, put it in black plastic garbage bags and loaded it into the jeep. I went back and gathered some brush and broken twigs. I strew them around the stone to give the appearance that it hadn't been recently laid, hoping that the grass would quickly push through and blend in the area in order to avoid detection.

The job was done. I stood over Ethan's grave and prayed. I thanked God for his memory, and once again I began to cry. I cried myself into another of those uncontrollable spells of torrentially flowing tears. Beneath the ground where my friend lay, I prayerfully whispered to him: "You

101

didn't think that I was going to leave you out here, nameless, with no stone to indicate that you ever lived or died, did you, my brother?"

Laying the stone gave me the assurance that the mortal remains of my best friend could now be found, no more guessing, no more making lines in the snow or dirt. I was comforted that if the angels flew over Barsdale, they could look down and readily identify the whereabouts of one of God's choice children. While less expensive than upright ones, maybe flat stones aren't in the inferior class of death and burial rituals, after all, because their writing can be easily seen from high above the earth. For big, upright and more expensive stones, you must be down of the ground to read them. You must *get down* to see them.

I returned home, feeling lifted and reconnected to Ethan's memory, humming a song of praise, ". . . I feel alright, no condemnation . . . in my soul today, no condemnation in my soul today . . ." The road to putting an honorable name and face back on him was still on course.

But my celebration wouldn't last. In one of his frequent visits to the cemetery, Norton discovered the stone. Who, how, and when it was laid piqued his concern. Unlike the friends of Jesus, curious as to who had rolled the stone away from his tomb, Norton wanted to know who had laid one at Ethan's. After eliminating members of his family, and a few of Ethan's friends, I was the thought to be the one most likely to have done it, a conjecture to which I proudly raise my hand. It was I.

Having a hunch that something had happened at Barsdale, a few weeks later I drove to Pittsfield and visited the gravesite. I was informed that the stone had been cracked into an infinite number of granite particles. I could see that it had been removed. If the person who beat and uprooted it hoped that I would be upset, they were right. This disregard and dastardly act of cracking it bordered on the unforgivably hideous. Removing it was one thing, but breaking it up and desecrating its spiritually intended purpose was another—to me. It was an ultimate insult to Ethan's death, not dissimilar to the many in his life, where he was broken into so many unfitting pieces, so dejected that his will to resist the forces of ridicule betrayed him.

I couldn't help but think of all the noises pounding *at* Ethan in life, and *over* him in death—from the loud banging accusations he heard from his home and church on his unfitness, to the click, click lock sounds on the bedroom door adjacent to his. There were those of the grave attendants with their clanging shovels and backhoes filling the hole over his coffin, then my spading and thumping the dirt to lay the first stone, followed by its vicious beating and cracking. Why, it was enough to wake all of Barsdale's dead. Maybe it did.

Of course, Ethan couldn't hear this commotion at all, could he? For, from the moment his head slumped over into his daughter's arms, when the plug to the machine pumping oxygen into his lungs was snatched out of the wall the following day, all he could hear were glory sounds. "Up above my head, I hear music in the air . . . " "Holy, Holy, Holy" and "Worthy Is the Lamb." He himself had joined this heavenly choir, a singing throng whose membership is so large that it cannot be numbered; and for the first time, and much to the delight of those in his section, he was singing in key.

I, on the other hand, was singing a different tune. Mine was the deeply pained disharmony that the body of my brother once again lay unidentified in a remote area out on the backside of Barsdale Cemetery. He lay in a place where men couldn't leave roses at his feet, where women couldn't drop off a plant and where children couldn't dust falling tree cones and wind-blown leaves from a stone bearing his name. None of them could walk up to his grave and say, "I love and miss you," because they wouldn't know exactly where his body lay.

Ten days later in Atlanta, I ran into one of Ethan's friends, Paula Higgins, who said that people in Pittsfield were bent out of shape because of a stone someone had anonymously laid at Ethan's grave. "Did you do it," she asked? When I inquired as to why she wanted to know, she indicated that she had been requested to ask me. Not fully trusting her motives, I gave her a misleading reply. The conversation ended with her telling me that I would be pleasantly surprised to know that Mrs. Lam was showing signs of really missing Ethan since his death, that she loved him now more than ever. This revelation was, indeed, a surprise, but there was nothing pleasant about it. How interesting, I thought, how interesting— *if only* . . .

I went to Barsdale again and discovered a military-made replacement monument, something I had known that the government freely does for soldiers at the request of surviving spouses or parents. All that is required is the presentation of an official military discharge and about five minutes for doing the paperwork. It is routine. While I don't think that gravestone aesthetics reflect anything about the character of those whose names they bear, the first stone—if I must say—speaks more to the brightness of Ethan's life, the second, to the cold, calculating designs to shade that life from honor and respect.

In any case, *if only* the military stone had been laid earlier . . . The baser part of me said I should remove it and install yet another one, making for musical chairs (stones). But, of course, that would have been the ultimate desecration, wouldn't it? My less than baser self said not to, to leave it. I did.

I have never asked Barsdale people of the first stone's whereabouts. I suspect, like all of those things that adorned Ethan's life with a modicum of recognition and dignity, it was heaped, maybe lying somewhere near those bags of garbage containing his clothes that were put out on the curb for collection two days after his burial. I think if I ever retrieve it from this heap, cracks and all, I will take it to the Gambia and place it on our mission grounds there, right next to a larger memorial rock on which I have had Ethan's name carved. Or maybe I'll put it in Sunyani, Ghana soil where we are building our next mission station or in Guinea-Bissau or Guinea, places on our agenda after that. We will see. On either of these fertile stretches of earth, where he pledged to come and work with me, and where our forefathers and foremothers birthed us in the belly of creation, it would be a fitting memorial to his tragic death and triumphant life.

This is that part of the story that addresses the *stones surrounding* Reverend Ethan Lam, Jr. where I sought to retrieve the account of his life and death from the crucibles of shame. That part having to do with *raising the saint inside* him is a fundamentally different one. It has little to do with rectifying legacy and history. It's transcendent, and has everything to do with his divinely appointed presence on earth, his sainthood.

Raising the Saint

Ethan's remarkably holy life was evidenced by the formidable strength with which he countersigned the bombardment of his afflictions, those that ungrudgingly scratched and gnawed their way into his soul. He did so with love, grace and mercy. He looked and sounded like that roster of individuals designated as righteous in the Bible, those in whom God found favor and imputed it—the ark builder, the patriarch and matriarch, the deliverer and the king, the prophet and the virgin. Ethan could have been numbered among them, or he could have been a modern Joseph, a young man to whom the angel came and said, "God is pleased with you. But you, Ethan, must weather some terrible episodes of scandal and punishment from those you cherish the most, your church, and your family."

Jesus was born to a poor couple from Nazareth. The Bible says, in John's Gospel, "He came unto His own, and His own received Him not; but to as many as received Him, to them gave He the power to become the sons of God." Ethan was born to poor Georgia and Alabama parents, descendants of slaves. He grew up a virgin until marriage and was a celibate when he died. He was called to be a minister of the gospel, a calling he faithfully carried out for more than forty years. He accepted the challenge to pastor his own, those at Mt. Holly Baptist Church, the community of faith in which he grew up. But its members were divided on who he was and his qualifications to lead them. They ultimately rejected him. He then spread the word of truth to as many people as would give him opportunity, all over Pittsfield and beyond.

Ethan was like the Hebrew, Hosea, the faithful and religious husband who loved his wife so much that she could do nothing to make him love her less, even if consistently found in violation of their sacred covenant. As Christ died for His imperfect bride, the church, who had gone away from His repeated beckoning for her to come close, Ethan died for his wayward bride. Actually, he died for both of them, his personal bride, who told him to go away, and his church bride who told him to—to go away. He continued to woo them because of his love.

Jesus wasn't born in His own house, nor buried in His own tomb. He was scandalized and bruised beyond recognition. His accusers trumped up false charges against Him and were curiously moot when asked to justify their actions. At any cost, and without basis, they just wanted to get rid of Him. Surprisingly, even to His followers, He chose not to deal with them with physical instruments of battle, but rather with heavenly ones: love, grace, and mercy. When He died, the curtain in the temple was rent, torn from top to bottom.

Reverend Ethan Lam, Jr.'s life was diminished to a spectacle of the worse kind of humiliation, so unjustifiably mangled that even his closest friends could hardly make out his identity. He extended *Shalom* to his adversaries, but to no avail. After his death, his remains were deposited in a wooden coffin and disgracefully placed in a six-foot nameless divide on the backside of a graveyard. A stone was made and placed over his remains, only to be deliberately cracked from side to side, from top to bottom, and uprooted.

Ethan could have made violent choices to battle his opponents, including the violence of having left his wife. He chose neither. Following the teachings of the books of Titus and I and II Timothy, regarding the credentials of being a spiritual leader, he deeply believed in the construct, one husband to one wife until death. He was not perfect, but he was blameless, as these epistles instruct that pastors should be. No one could point a finger at him as a willful violator of the commandments of God.

Some theologians have argued that the cause of Jesus' death was as much moral as it was physical: that He died of a broken heart. In addition to the unimaginable pain caused by crucifixion, a common form of execution at this time, Jesus, an innocent man, was bearing the weight of the sins of the world, causing Him this moral death that speedied up His physical demise.

Ethan was innocent of the charges thrown in his face and may have similarly lost his battle to live, due to moral collapse. He had been rejected and unnecessarily accused long enough, had had his share of disappointment, betrayal and abuse long enough. His terminal physical incapacitation, when his heart refused to beat another beat and his lungs inhale another breath, may have, indeed, been precipitated by a prior and irreversible bruising of his will. In sum, his death was a moral crucifixion—his burial, unscrupulous and shameless.

In raising his sainthood, these citations are not intended to be a blasphemous hermeneutic of Scripture. Most certainly, Ethan was not the Christ and would reject any referendum to bring the events of his life anywhere near those of Jesus. I have simply drawn these parallels to show that he was a follower of God, and was one of those special people sent to enter and leave our world, that in his journey he was called on to endure suffering to bring us closer to God. I think he was saint.

Not all agree with this review of Ethan's life. I recently asked someone who knew him, and who strongly challenged my assertion that he was a saint, if she had in the more than forty years she had known him ever witnessed him doing anything wrong, or ever heard a report from someone else that he had? She said, "No." Of all the pastors she had had over a fifty-year period, I asked if any had paid her more pastoral visits than Ethan (and he was never her pastor)? Her answer was no, again. Regarding whether we should think or not think that he was a saint, I then said this might be a good place to start making an intelligent determination.

One Pittsfielder, a friend of Ethan, actually suggested that he was cowardly and unable to decisively act against his attackers. But nothing could be further from the truth. Ethan was a paragon of courage. If his fight appeared weak, it's only because his weapons were spiritual, not carnal, the thinking level of those drawing such a conclusion. There is no way to explain the unbreakable allegiance he had to his moral principles, otherwise.

I suspect that after cleaning out the desk and file cabinets, most of us would have backed up the U-Haul to the church door and loaded in our belongings and moved on without hesitation, as some suggested that Ethan should have done. But he opted to stay, not as a confrontational combatant, but as soldier of the cross. Despite the irreparable cracks in his contractual and covenantal marriages, he remained faithful, even to death.

In today's political marketplace so ostensibly concerned with the future of our youth, the call for wholesome role models and mentors is frequently the lead story. (Regrettably, it's often disingenuous journalistic hype.) On the real side, I offer Ethan Lam, Jr. We can name our children and streets after him, illustrate him in our speeches on faithfulness and consistency, and preach his life of Christian obedience, tolerance, and forgiveness in our sermons.

Ethan Lam, Jr. always opened and closed his days with prayer and reading the Scriptures. He was so in love with Jesus that what he wanted mostly was for others to know Him. To invite them to make His acquaintance was as easy to him as sharing love, as a baby crying, as *touch a leaf and see the sky* . . . It is an invitation that preceded and has survived him, one that will outlast all us earthly mortals headed for our own New Year's Eve, shall we say, "great gettin' up mornin . . . " It remains an open one in this testimony of him, here and now, *right where I stand.*

Contrary to those who sent cautionary signals to me about meddling with Ethan's soul and memory, disturbing his state of tranquility, as I said, it was never a question of whether they rest in peace. It was always a matter of his life, his death and his legacy resting there, without distortion and ridicule. Now that that is the case, may the memory of Ethan Lam, Jr. *live* in peace. Finally, forgiveness was the calling card that he left with those who abused him. It was a redeeming virtue branded in him with the same tongs of fire touching Isaiah's lips nearly 3,000 years ago. I hope that after the dust has settled from this record, after the anger from its revelations has subsided, when some of Pittsfield's clergy have condemned the story in their preachments and after I have been summonsed by the authorities to discuss my laying the stone, that Ethan's marred legacy will take its place in the archives of the glorious saints. It is my hope that whether or not I am forever held in contempt by those taking issue with "Who Will *Lay* The First Stone . . . ?" may the Spirit of the living God, as manifested in Reverend Ethan Lam, Jr., define the terms upon which we find reconciliation, peace and forgiveness.

Postscript

(A City Set on a Hill . . .)

The city we grew up in and loved appears so excessively transformed beyond its natural and social evolution. Once enthusiastic and lively environments for the expression of culture and religion, Pittsfield's black neighborhoods now appear listless and sterile. Sprawling expressways and shopping malls have altered its street gymnasiums and its neighborhood conviviality. Robust, intelligent African American men who worked in the rubber and car factories to fuel the nation's industrial economy, in curiously high numbers, now spend inordinate amounts of time in pool halls, coffee houses, and beer taverns. Their conversations center on arduously held positions as to which cars are the best made, fastest, and most durable. As they had done when younger, at the old custard stand, they continue to shine and groom these prized models on Saturday and Sunday mornings, displaying them as symbols of success and their own location in Pittsfield's social order. The old Cadillac has maintained its high ranking as *the* car to have, while BMW's, Mercedes Benz's, and Saab's are the preferred models of their educated sons and daughters.

Perhaps I shouldn't be so hard on my friends, because they have little to link them to the world out of which they came. Their high school idols no longer rumble up and down Pennsylvania's football fields, untouched by human hands seeking to break their strides, if not their legs. Their political leaders lack the moral courage of their predecessors, to rebuild and take the city into its future. They can no longer witness boys kiss girls in the streets, a sign of their

111

love, but rather helplessly watch them shoot and kill them there, a sign of their hate. Or, is it a sign of the times?

Pittsfield is not the same because Marti doesn't sing our hearts happy now. Where is she, anyway? Oh, I think I see her standing over there in a choir loft next to Sister Juella, a woman whose quivering soprano voice we used to hear in the front row of the senior choir at St. James Church. As children, we laughed when she sang. We were silly and disrespectful. If only we could hear her sing again, Pittsfield would surely be a better choir in which to blend our own quivering voices.

I know that Queen Esther's place is forever closed for house parties, and to those who want to drop in to *dance to the music.* Where her house used to be is now a neighborhood dumping site.

And where are those heavy summer rains that once pitter-pattered Pittfield's streets, melodiously harmonizing the sounds of giggling children slapping their bare feet on the steamy sidewalks, while soothingly warm waters ran along the trenches, trickling between their dirty toes?

And, oh! Is that a blimp in the sky, or is that a bomb I see?

The old Pittsfield may have just floated out to Simmel Beach Lake, because its smooth-talkin' brothers are not around to seductively charm the sisters, and Edo Denson's 1949 white Mercury has long since been melted down to make barbed wire fences for prisons and school yards. Willow trees on Abin Avenue don't hang low enough to shelter the innocent embrace of teenage lovers like they once did, always under the careful watch of their parents peeking through the window. Can we trust him with our daughter? they then asked. They concluded later, they couldn't.

Where is the old skating rink? Is it true that it is now a residential compound for the elderly?

112

Dudes from neighboring Kentley have stopped shooting jump shots at Roosevelt High, and word has it that they abandoned the beauty queens of their hometown and found that Pittsfield had some worth pursuing. The road to their beloved Kentley is now closed, and Hollie, Skates, and Raymond, their star players, are dead. It seems that basketball wizards, Jethro and Henry, have stopped dazzling crowds in Pekins Woods with their play, while Gus Jackson's death brought the sports' community to a grinding halt. Is that why Pittsfield is so changed? Fourth of July barbecue smoke that once ascended so far and high that residents could identify their own hog fumes from distant miles doesn't rise so high, now. And grape Kool Aid is no longer a nickel. How we got a whole gallon from one pack I will never know. Maybe we used it just to color our sugar water, creating the illusion that dinner was ready and it was time to grease.

Hector's and Ike's are now big empty lots on the "avenue," distant reminders of their one-time solidifying community functions, and Bobby J. can't slap us in the face just because he wants to any longer. Actually, we really don't miss bad Bobby's use of brute power to subjugate the already frightfully weak. We really don't. When Myrtle Brooks was around, and he went on his "rambo" rampages, she could always talk him out of a throw-down. The many times I was on the run because word had it that he sought to turn my lights out, I welcomed her intervention.

Louis D. Wimsly is not shaking the dance floor when doing the shuffle to ". . . You Give Me Fever" these days. He is now Dr. Wimsly, having joined his old friends, Drs. Lee and Green. They are all wonderfully choreographing the lives of children and youth in educational arenas, teaching them to get it off on some new possibilities these days. These brothers are model examples of what the city was, along with sisters Clissie, Sandra, Mayme, Joyce, and Bettie.

In the aftermath of Ethan's death, it is just so hard to reconstruct a smiling image of the city, that city on the hill, a once expansive oasis of hope. It appears to be surrounded by islands of polluted wasteland for too many of its children to wander aimlessly in, those for whom the sun doesn't shine as bright, nor is the snow as white and as much fun for them to play in outside. Nintendo culture, Game Boy, Play Stations, and the Internet have created a false sense of more valid recreation and learning for them inside. A pity.

When walking Pittsfield's streets, riding its avenues and running its alleys, there are few evidences of those times when you spoke to people on their porch as you passed by, and they spoke back. Gone are the days when children went out of their way to help an elderly person struggling with a bag of groceries on the other side of the street, when saying "yes, mam" and "no, sir" was not viewed as aging those greeted or the greeting itself. It was just a cultural matter of respect. It was a cultural *thang,* a good *thang.*

I was recently back in the city looking for our house on Livings Street, and for the driveway where I used to window-gaze at those coming and leaving Mrs. Walker's. I stood many a day in that big old gray dwelling, shivering over the furnace vent, trying to keep warm in the winter. That had to be the coldest house in Pennsylvania. But trying to find the old family dwelling was useless. The whole neighborhood has been lifted out of the earth and put somewhere else. I wish I knew where.

Mrs. Dixon's store is closed now, as are 95 percent of Pittfield's neighborhood grocery outlets. Where are the days when their friendly clerks gave you a quart of milk and half pound of longhorn cheese with a smile? Fed's car wash is but a memory, along with Friday night house parties and Saturday night mixers—or is it the other way around?

Aunt Pinkie is now dead. Who will go to bat for us to get jobs and for a little self-confidence when we feel shy and reserved? Speck's Supermarket is out of business, and I cannot steal lemons for Mayme Ruth from its fruit bins. And even if I could, she is dead now.

Could space aliens have played a cruel hoax on Pittsfield, sneaked in and abducted its inspiration and dream makers while the rest of the city slept?

Worcester Avenue Temple, now Bishop Ash Temple named after its illustrious pastor, is not that red shingled building on the corner of Worcester and Belmont anymore. Once addressing the needs of the whole community, this church significantly impacted us. It made low-income apartments available for some of our poor. It fed us bacon, eggs, and freshly made biscuits on Sunday mornings, and potato pies, cornbread, and collard greens on Sunday afternoons. If we returned Sunday evenings, when hearing its drum and guitar section beat out rhythms of holiness, we would be provided stirring preachments, food for the soul.

It has now moved upon the hill. I'm not sure of its religious and social relevancy these days, or of its food menus since being up there. I do know that migration up on the hill—that's "Sugar Hill"—usually means that folks preach and praise differently, even if they eat the same. They start looking more inside to the needs of themselves than outside to those of others. As I said, I am not sure.

And Providence Baptist Church, that little wooden church sitting back off Rancon Street, that comfortably packed in one hundred more people than it could possibly hold, has a new look, I hear. I remember that it used to get so crowded and hot at Providence in the summer that you couldn't even raise your hand to fan your face, yet there was always room in the aisles to shout. I drove by looking for it the other day. Where is it, and the Pittsfield that gave it birth?

Has the city spun off its axis because the apostolic voices of the old-time religion are now quiet, replaced with a group of preaching professionals who bring corporate values to our churches when negotiating contracts? It is reported that they seduce poor congregations to give them a standard of living far beyond their means, poor congregations, that is—big salaries, expensive cars, posh parsonages, extra pay for visiting the sick, *everythang*. Unconscionable.

Pittsfield's African American churches are now sharply divided. *It hurts so bad* to witness it. Rarely is there worship and cooperation between them, albeit, an occasional anniversary and program event. As America's social elite differentiate themselves by the country clubs, resorts, golf courses, and families they play and marry in, Pittsfield's big churches have developed exclusive intramural clubs of their own. They and their members wrap each other in cloaks of superiority and distinction, peeking condescendingly over the rims of their designer glasses at their erstwhile church kin. Smaller congregations are no better, are, in fact, equally to blame for this syndrome of separate and unequal union. All too often they genuflect with self-inflicted wounds of inferiority, acquiescing to the defense that being little in size is the price they are *called* to pay for their divinely conferred status as the true believers.

I hear that campaigns of religious separatism are being waged against those not sympathetic to the views of their advocates, that the latter's zealot pontifications of intolerance and exclusivity can be heard above the old voices of reason and love. The Pittsfield African American church may have just become a place where her once cherished elderly are her latest casualties, a dark sanctuary where ritualized preachments bore her youth and cold basements where her children are being snatched into religious oblivion. Paradoxically, these are the youth and children that so much rhetorical attention is given to in Sunday morning preachments,

116

targets of relentless condemnations and disingenuous curiosity, such as "... What has happened to our youth ...?"

While the "back in the day" Pittsfield church was surely the foundation upon which the community stood for its vision and direction, it has sadly become the cracks through which many seeking salvation and assurance are *slipping into darkness* and stumbling into disillusionment. Once heralded as a haven of salvation for the lost and hope for the downtrodden, it has become a smokescreen for misappropriating financial resources, of cronyism and hype, a place so feebly obsessed with the fickle and mundane that the cycle of its nihilism is irresolute.

Maybe the city's mothers and fathers need to recall the persuasive homiletics of those moral trumpeters mentioned above, those whose teachings on wholeness and holiness were like morning mists, gently falling on our scorched and tired souls. If only her new clerics would craft their leadership modalities at the feet of these architects of integrity, our churches might be stronger, our streets safer, our families more stable, our civics more honorable, and our children still ours. Perhaps then, we would truly fellowship with each other again, no matter the congregational size, its social, racial, or theological makeup. Perhaps.

Ethan's mother is preparing to move out of Pittsfield to live with her daughter in the Midwest, I hear. I told her that if Ethan were alive, he wouldn't let her do so. She agreed. Mother Lam is not well, I understand, and she needs the loving care of her daughter. I went to Pittsfield for the last time to be with her. When I got to the house, I made a final pilgrimage through it. Now old and squeaky, and looking remarkably smaller than back in the day, I walked in those rooms in which we once bathed our thoughts, dreams, and relationships. I did so in a slow, deliberate, and sanctified stroll, recapturing joyous moments of its inestimable meanings of our past.

Mother Lam prepared me a sweet potato pie, which I ate in its entirety before reaching New York the next day, necessitating a few unscheduled rest-area stops, en route. She also fixed me some cornbread and collard greens. I mixed, sopped, and ate them with my fingers, meticulously licking each one with delight, as though there was no tomorrow. In fact, that's how I felt: that there was no tomorrow, that I would never see Mother Lam again and break her bread on *this side of the Jordan River*. I relished every moment in her presence. I suspect that Pittsfield will continue looking dreadfully unfamiliar, if not lost, in her absence.

In conclusion, Pittsfield is really not the same because Reverend Ethan Lam, Jr. is dead, that young emblem of grace whose triumphant engagement with the angels of darkness has forever affected the way some of us think and behave. His saintly life will remain deeply engrained in our memories, as will the good fight of faith that he so gallantly fought until breathing his last breath. Unless the steel city and those who so recklessly toyed with his sojourn revisit his life and death, things will never be right in Pittsfield. On the other hand, if they do, *it could once again be that city set upon a hill that cannot be hid . . .*